Another Me

ALSO BY HEATHER DUERRE HUMANN

Gender Bending Detective Fiction: A Critical Analysis of Selected Works (McFarland, 2017)

Domestic Abuse in the Novels of African American Women: A Critical Study (McFarland, 2014)

Another Me

The Doppelganger in 21st Century Fiction, Television and Film

Heather Duerre Humann

McFarland & Company, Inc., Publishers
Jefferson, North Carolina

LIBRARY OF CONGRESS CATALOGUING-IN-PUBLICATION DATA

Names: Humann, Heather Duerre, 1974– author.
Title: Another me : the doppelganger in 21st century fiction, television and film / Heather Duerre Humann.
Description: Jefferson, North Carolina : McFarland & Company, Inc., Publishers, 2018. | Includes bibliographical references and index.
Identifiers: LCCN 2017053062 | ISBN 9781476671765 (softcover : acid free paper) ∞
Subjects: LCSH: Doubles in mass media. | Doubles in literature. | Fiction—21st century—History and criticism.
Classification: LCC P96.D65 H86 2018 | DDC 809/.927—dc23
LC record available at https://lccn.loc.gov/2017053062

BRITISH LIBRARY CATALOGUING DATA ARE AVAILABLE

ISBN 978-1-4766-7176-5 (print)
ISBN 978-1-4766-3172-1 (ebook)

© 2018 Heather Duerre Humann. All rights reserved

No part of this book may be reproduced or transmitted in any form or by any means, electronic or mechanical, including photocopying or recording, or by any information storage and retrieval system, without permission in writing from the publisher.

Front cover photograph by Jeff Bergen (iStock)

Printed in the United States of America

McFarland & Company, Inc., Publishers
 Box 611, Jefferson, North Carolina 28640
  www.mcfarlandpub.com

To my beautiful children, Ashley and James.
You two are my whole world.
I love you both with all my heart.

Table of Contents

Acknowledgments ix
Introduction: The Monster in the Mirror 1

Section I. Literature 21
  1. Twinning in Audrey Niffenegger's *Her Fearful Symmetry* 27
  2. The Pursuit of Self? José Saramago's *The Double* 35
  3. The Ethics of Cloning in Kazuo Ishiguro's *Never Let Me Go* 42
  4. Through a Machine Darkly: Blake Crouch's *Dark Matter* 50
  5. Technology and the Self in Dexter Palmer's *Version Control* 58
  6. Clones (and Crime) in Space: Mur Lafferty's *Six Wakes* 65

Section II. Television and Film 75
  7. The Twin Formula in *Ringer* and *The Lying Game* 81
  8. The Motif of the Double in *Fringe* and *Battlestar Galactica* 86
  9. *Westworld*, the 21st Century Technoculture Take on Doubles 98
 10. Clones and Cultural Anxieties in *Orphan Black* 112
 11. Cinematic Clones in *The Island* and *Oblivion* 122
 12. Monstrous Doubling and Magical Illusion in *The Prestige* 136

Conclusion: Cultural Anxieties and Doppelgangers in the 21st Century 151
Bibliography 159
Index 167

Acknowledgments

This book, like most creative and critical works, drew inspiration from many people. In fact, I am certain that this book would not have been possible without the support of my family, friends, colleagues, mentors, and publisher. My wish is to therefore express my sincere gratitude to those who have helped me along the way.

First, I must communicate my profound gratitude to my family for providing me with support and encouragement throughout the process of researching and writing this book. Above all, I want to say thanks to my two beautiful children, Ashley and James, who mean the world to me. To them, I would like to say that everything I accomplish and work toward is so that you will be as proud of me as I am of you both. I also want to express appreciation to my sweet husband, Madison, for his love and support. Kind thanks are also due to my grandmother, Alice Duerre, who has always been a source of support and encouragement. I would like to thank my dad, Jim Duerre. I also appreciate the support of my father-in-law, Phil Humann.

I would like, as well, to communicate my appreciation to the many friends, colleagues, and mentors who have provided me ideas, support, conversation, and encouragement at various points along the way. This list includes Marion Eckert (and her lovely family), Bonnie Whitener, Stephanie Cobb, Cathy Skinner (a great running partner), Dianne Shaw Freeman (another great running partner), Kim Jackson, Linda Rowland, Molly Creeger, Evie Brown (a great workout partner), and Jonas Elliott (CrossFit coach and fitness trainer extraordinaire).

My experiences as a student at the University of Georgia, my time as both a student and faculty member at the University of Alabama, and my teaching experience at Shelton State College have done much to shape me as a scholar, writer, and academic, so I would also like to express appreciation to those institutions and the fine faculty and students there who encouraged and inspired me along the way. I am very fortunate to work and teach in a supportive environment, so I also need to express thanks to the Department of Language and Literature and the College of Arts and Sciences at Florida Gulf Coast University.

Introduction: The Monster in the Mirror

Popular music has recently relied on the motif of the "monster in the mirror" to bring questions related to identity into debate. A good example of this can be found in Usher's hit 2010 R&B song "More," which he co-wrote with Charles Hinshaw and RedOne (aka Nadir Khayat). In "More," Usher sings about being the monster in the mirror, thus alluding to having a shadow side and expressing dual feelings of fear and fascination with the self. In essence, Usher is speaking about having a double. A similar set of concerns can be found in "The Monster," a popular 2013 song performed by rap artist Eminem and featuring guest vocals from singer Rihanna. "The Monster," which was written by Eminem, Jon Bellion, and Bebe Rexha, includes lyrics which describe befriending the monster that is under the bed and getting along with the voices inside of one's own head. As an artist who created and frequently writes about his alter-ego (Slim Shady), Eminem reflects an awareness of both the tension and possibility tied to the proverbial "monster in the mirror." In fact, this is a hallmark feature of his oeuvre, so although "The Monster" is perhaps the song where he comes across as being most self-aware about his simultaneous fear of, and fascination with, the self, it is just one of many songs where Eminem addresses this theme.

Musical performers such as Usher, Eminem, and Rihanna are just a few of the many examples of contemporary artists who use creative works to explore identity-related questions by referencing their darker side. To be sure, these questions emerge in, and are at the heart of, much of popular culture. Indeed, in the 21st century, it is not only music, but also literary fiction, film, and television which frequently deploy the motif of the double (or doppelganger) to engage with issues related to identity, autonomy, and self-expression, notions which are being challenged, contested, and redefined in contemporary times. As a result, these ideas both reflect and produce a significant amount of cultural ambivalence for those of us living in the current era.

The motif of the doppelganger can be clearly seen in contemporary popular culture, but the concept is actually a very old one. A German term, *Doppelgänger* derives from *doppel* (meaning "duplicate" or "double") and *Gänger* (meaning "goer"); thus, the English word doppelganger (generally without the umlaut) literally means "double goer" (or "double walker") and the term refers to a double of a living person. While the word "doppelganger" derives from the late 18th century, examples of doppelgangers—or doubles—can be found in stories from both early Egypt and ancient Mesopotamia. For example, the double makes an appearance in Egyptian mythology (dating back to before the Common Era) through the figure of the ka', a "spirit double." Another case can be found in *The Epic of Gilgamesh*, an epic poem from Mesopotamian civilization (circa 2100 BCE), where the eponymous hero first battles and then later befriends his double. Accounts of doubles are also described in Norse folklore, through a being known as vardøger, a figure that appears as a ghostly double of a living human.

Image and Identity

While examples of doppelgangers can be traced back thousands of years, contemporary popular culture is also replete with examples of the figure, thus illustrating the fact that the doppelganger is both a timely and enduring image. As a perennial as well as durable image, the doppelganger continues to reemerge in various forms of cultural expression. What accounts for this? What are the reasons that the doppelganger has long held captive the human imagination through myths and stories? Why does this figure continue to reemerge in popular narratives?

The popularity of the figure derives, in large part, from the fact that the doppelganger is a cultural vehicle whose meaning has shifted over time. Donato Totaro argues in his 1998 article "The Contemporary Doppelgänger" that the "influx of doppelgänger imagery reinvents and mirrors itself," thus suggesting the "inexhaustibility of the doppelgänger" figure. Indeed, the theme of the doppelganger has been one of the most "persistent in all the arts" (Totaro). An image related to identity and the search for the self, the figure of the doppelganger reflects timeless preoccupations. For instance, the double has frequently been relied upon to represent an individual's internal psychological struggles. Traditionally, the figure also has been deployed to highlight fears about the self and the other.

The motif of the doppelganger continues to reflect many of these same concerns today, but in the case of the 21st century, there are new implications related to the figure, as well, ones which remain tied to both changing cultural norms and emerging technologies. For many people living in the 21st century, these emerging forms of media and technology offer new opportunities for frequent self-expression and even reinvention. This is due, in large part, to social and professional networking sites (like Twitter, Facebook, Google+, Instagram, and LinkedIn, to name just a few), which offer the freedom to actively construct an identity—or even different identities. Indeed, we now have the ability to self-fashion, that is, to consciously construct our identity and public persona in whichever way we choose.

The 21st century, however, also requires people to be adaptable in ways that previous generations did not have to be. Sherry Turkle explains this shift in her book *Life on the Screen: Identity in the Age of the Internet* (1995):

> Not so long ago, stability was socially valued and culturally reinforced. Rigid gender roles, repetitive labor, the expectation of being in one kind of job or remaining in one town over a lifetime, all of these made consistency central to definitions of self. But these stable social worlds have broken down. What matters most now is the ability to adapt and change—to new jobs, new career directions, new gender roles, new technologies [255].

So, while technology and new means of communication provide innovative ways to reinvent ourselves, the reality of contemporary times also pushes us to quickly adapt to different roles and rapidly advancing computer and communication technologies. One result is that there is a tension between these freedoms and the demands placed on us by such technology. In fact, as Turkle emphasizes, this brings with it a new dilemma: "How can we be multiple and coherent at the same time?" (258).

While there is little doubt that Sherry Turkle began an important conversation about the changing nature of identity in a postmodern world, in the decades since she first discussed the anxiety and promise of multiplicity, these concerns have taken different forms, as both technology and culture have continued to change and evolve. Since the time Turkle laid out her argument, debates related to identity have continued to rage— and, indeed, they are still very much playing out today. The storylines of many recent films and television programs reflect these controversies while also demonstrating an attitude shift about what it means to be human in the early 21st century.

In our contemporary era, a fundamental part of being human is our ability to adapt, change, and remain flexible, qualities which are mirrored (and also beneficial) in the many virtual realms (including social networking, online media, and the like) that are so prevalent today. As Kenneth Gergen, author of *The Saturated Self: Dilemmas of Identity in Contemporary Life*, argues, we have become the "possessors of many voices" (83). According the Gergen, in the contemporary era, we each have many selves: "Each self contains a multiplicity of others, singing different melodies, different verses, and with different rhythms. Nor do these many voices necessarily harmonize. At times they join together, at times they fail to listen one to another, and at times they create a jarring discord. But what are the consequences of the multiply populated self?" (83).

Though there are clear benefits to this model of multiplicity, there are real challenges, as well. As Elaine L. Graham notes in her book *Representations of the Post/Human: Monsters, Aliens, and Others in Popular Culture*, "identity in a cyberworld is fluid and negotiable," and, this fluidity can cause a "decentering" of self, an effect which (though it may be welcome by some individuals) may operate as a source of tension (191).

The growing sense that we are all becoming multiple, and the fact that we remain ambivalent about it, bears scrutiny because this reflects our fragmented, postmodern state of identity. However, in order to effectively address the 21st century cultural anxieties that are both projected onto, and reflected by, the figure of the doppelganger, it is necessary to first consider how the figure has historically been theorized.

A Psychological Study

In 1914, Otto Rank (1884–1939) wrote what is arguably the most famous psychological study of the double. An early Freudian psychoanalyst, Rank discusses the figure in his book *The Double: A Psychoanalytic Study (Der Doppelgänger: Eine Psychoanalytische Studie)*, where he highlights the connection between Sigmund Freud's theories of the unconscious and the doppelganger, an image that caught his attention (and gained in popularity) due to its prevalence in Germanic folklore, where it frequently took the form of a paranormal double of a living person. Rank explains that the figure of the double, at its root, represents disguised narcissistic self-love.

Rank, in fact, specifically references Narcissus, the notorious figure from Greek mythology, who obsesses over his own reflection up until the point that it consumes and thus kills him. While Rank considers how the figure appears in mythology, he also addresses the double as it appears in the physical world, discussing cases such as twins and mirror images, for example, and in superstition, citing the reluctance of primitive people to be photographed. The first to use the lens of psychoanalytic theory to address literary doppelgangers, Rank posits that since the fear of death is overwhelming, conceiving of the double is also a way to create a new self that will live on (he uses the example of Oscar Wilde's well-known 1890 novel, *The Picture of Dorian Gray*, whose main character's self-portrait—and double—does not age, as an example of this). Rank further argues that having a double is a way avoid responsibility for one's actions, since the individual could therefore claim his double is actually the one responsible for the misdeed.

As Otto Rank notes, the figure was also frequently associated with bad luck. For instance, many believed that the vision of a doppelganger by family members is said to foreshadow illness or impending danger, while when seen by oneself it becomes an omen of death. Individuals who claim to have seen their own double have oftentimes expressed fear that their encounter with a look-a-like portends some sort of misfortune.

Visions of Doppelgangers

Numerous accounts of visions of doppelgangers do, in fact, exist and, some of these can be found in the personal notes and letters of famous historical figures. For example, authors including the British renaissance poet, John Donne (1573–1631), the German writer, Johann Wolfgang von Goethe (1749–1832), and the British romantic novelist, Mary Wollstonecraft Shelley (1779–1851), who writes of her husband's many alleged encounters with his own double, have all penned such accounts. The case of the poet Percy Bysshe Shelley (1792–1822) is particularly interesting, since he claimed to have seen his own doppelganger shortly before his death.

In 1822, Percy Shelley drowned (as the result of a sailing accident), but prior to his death, he confessed to his wife Mary Shelley that he had met his double many times. Mary Shelley relayed this information in a letter she penned to Maria Gisborne (Bennett 245). According to the account she gave, these encounters included one particularly haunting experience when Percy Shelley walked out onto a terrace, only to be met by his doppelganger who asked him, "How long do you mean to be content?" As accounts such as the one Percy and Mary Shelley reported suggests, the doppelganger has been frequently understood as a superstitious figure.

Storytelling and Doubles

Historically, various forms of doubles (whether doppelgangers, twins, or some other type of look-a-like) have indeed caused both fear and fascination, and, as far back as there have been stories, the figure has existed. Doubles have made their way into mythology, religion, literature, and other forms of cultural expression. From Castor and Pollux, the twin brothers from Greek mythology and the basis for the constellation Gemini, to the epic tales of the Hero Twins in the sacred ancient Mayan text known as *Popol Vuh*, to William Shakespeare (1564–1616), himself the father of boy-girl twins (his twins, born in 1585, were named Hamnet and Judith Shakespeare), who, time and again, relied upon the concept of twins and doubling in his plays, and to Edgar Allan Poe (1809–1849), whose short fiction features the trend of doubles, the figure has long-fascinated humankind.

In William Shakespeare's literary works, the motif of the double is, in fact, a frequent and recurring one. As Daisy Garofalo highlights in "Shakespeare's Twins," he "features twin characters in two of his comedies, *The Comedy of Errors* (1593) and *Twelfth Night* (1601)," thus "capitalizing on the potential for mistaken identity and misdirected affection that twin likeness offers" in these plays. The example of the *Comedy of Errors* is of particular interest since it traces the adventures of two sets of identical twins who were separated at birth.

The play details how Antipholus and his manservant Dromio (both of Syracuse) travel to Ephesus, where they encounter their twin brothers, who are also named Antipholus and Dromio. Although *The Comedy of Errors* has all of the makings of a tragedy—the play follows a series of mishaps based on mistaken identities, including false accusations, beatings, a near-seduction, theft, madness, possession, and a wrongful arrest—by its end, the play has taken a comic turn and its ends with families being reunited. Indeed, as Kent Cartwright go as far as to say in his Introduction to the Arden Shakespeare edition of the play, "joy dominates *Errors'* conclusion" (49).

While *The Comedy of Errors* boasts a happy ending, not all storylines that involve twins or doubles can do so. Take the case of the short fiction of American writer Edgar Allan Poe. Much like Shakespeare, Poe consistently relied upon the motif of the double in his literary works, developing the theme perhaps most overtly in his story "William Wilson" (1839). Like Shakespeare's *The Comedy of Errors*, Poe's "William Wilson" remains focused on identity issues; however, while the many problems in *The Comedy of Errors*, a play centered on the notion of misidentification, get happily resolved when everyone learns their true identities, Poe's "William Wilson" ends tragically.

In "William Wilson," the narrator learns that a fellow classmate shares with him not only the name William Wilson, but also the same build, style of dress, and vocal intonation. The fear of losing his identity eventually pushes the narrator to murder his double, but his actions also bring about his own death. According to William E. Engel, who discusses the story in his book *Early Modern Poetics in Melville and Poe: Memory, Melancholy, and the Emblematic Tradition*, part of Poe's inspiration for the story was his desire to express the horror one feels when discovering another person shares "the same name" (85).

In the case of "William Wilson," the two men "also share the same birthday, January 19, which happens also to be Poe's birthday" (Engel 85). Engel further suggests that Poe's use of the doppelganger figure in this story reflects the anxiety associated with the search for self and identity, arguing that the story implies a sort of "degenerative self-duplication," which is echoed by the name "William Wilson" since "Wilson" sounds like "Will's son" (81).

Like William E. Engel, Robert T. Tally, Jr., who discusses the story "William Wilson" in his book *Poe and the Subversion of American Literature*, also argues that Poe's use of the figure of the doppelganger is connected to questions about identity and self-expression (Tally's reading, however, focuses most heavily on the story's beginning and end). With respect to how the story begins, he argues that there is what he terms as a "dual identification and nonidentification of the narrator" since he "declines give his real name" and, instead, only "provisionally introduces himself" by using a pseudonym, thus obscuring his identity (Tally 118). Tally also provides a close reading of the story's final scene, offering an interpretation of Wilson's murder of his double—and act which brings about his own death. Tally specifically highlights the role of the mirror in the room, thus calling attention to how the story relies on the notion of doubling from start to finish.

A story that relies upon the concept of doubling to explore identity, Poe's "William Wilson" tests, at the same time as it troubles, boundaries. As Christopher Joseph Gerrick explains in "Fear of the In-Between:

Interstitial Space in Edgar Allan Poe's 'William Wilson,'" the story is about boundaries, not only because of the distinction between the self and the other (meaning between William Wilson and his doppelganger), but also in the way these boundaries break down.

Alongside the themes that Engel, Tally, and Gerrick address in their readings of "William Wilson," it is worth noting, as well, that the story rather conspicuously reflects the sentiment that "you are your own worst enemy"—especially because of the manner in which the story ends, with both the narrator and his rival's death. Indeed, in these and other ways, Poe's treatment of the double in "William Wilson" calls attention to the anxiety that has long-been associated with the figure of the double. Moreover, the story hints to the likely sources of this anxiety: the fear of self and the fear of annihilation.

Looking at Edgar Allan Poe's story side-by-side with William Shakespeare's play reveals both the parallels and differences between the ways these authors' literary works engage with the figure of the double. Despite their obvious differences, both authors' texts are noteworthy because of the important roles they play in the long existence of the literary trope of the doppelganger. Though neither author was the first to rely on the figure of the double, both authors nonetheless helped to cement the doppelganger as a significant figure in literature (especially considering the literary preeminence of both Shakespeare and Poe). Moreover, both authors, by relying on the figure in their literary works, helped to establish (albeit different) formulas for how the durable figure might function within literature. In the case of both William Shakespeare and Edgar Allan Poe, the inclusion of the figure of the double as a motif also raises interesting questions about the nature of identity.

Literary works such as these push readers to ask: What is identity? Does it exist merely as the combination of competing forces (our memories and experiences, perhaps), or does it represent something distinct? Is identity merely an iterative act, or is there more to identity than simply performing identity? Questions such as these have long-plagued storytellers who, in turn, have relied on the figure of the doppelganger to explore debates about identity, individualism, autonomy, agency, and human rights.

Today, these same debates are still playing out. Indeed, in recent years, there has been an outpouring of storylines that involve twins, doubles, clones, or some other form of doppelganger. The popularity of these narratives reveal our preoccupation with individualism, a concept which is being challenged at the same time as new spaces are being made in which we can explore and experiment with identity. Indeed, while it is true that the figure of the double has long held captive the human imagination through myths and stories, the function and symbolic currency bound together with many contemporary representations of twins and doppelgangers are rife with new meanings, meanings tied directly to growing cultural norms and emerging technologies. As a products of popular culture, novels, television programs, and films provide lenses through which to consider identity-related questions. Examining how the figure appears in these different forms of popular culture opens up a space for comparison between how the doppelganger figure has traditionally been deployed versus how the motif typically emerges in the contemporary era.

Traditional representations of the doppelganger tend to share much in common. As Andrew J. Webber outlines in his book *The Doppelgänger: Double Visions in German Literature*, there exist various components to the archetypal figure which include visual, speech, and performative aspects. With respect to the visual, in "doppelgänger texts," the "subject beholds its other self as another, as visual object, or alternatively is beheld by object by its other self" (Webber 3). However, not only does the figure operate on a visual level, but it "operates divisively on language" because it "echoes, reiterates, distorts, parodies, dictates, impedes, and dumbfounds the subjective faculty of free speech" (Webber 3). Moreover, the figure exists as an "inveterate performer of identity," and also functions as a figure of "displacement" since it also characteristically "appears out of place, in order to displace its host" (Webber 3–4).

Contemporary representations of the figure hearken back to these traditional ways that the archetypal figure has tended to operate, but they also take on new significance—specifically, they emphasize the fluidity and malleability of identity in a cyberworld. Depictions in the 21st century thus rely on the history of the doppelganger while also pushing their audiences to consider the contemporary cultural anxieties brought to light by the figure of the double. At the same time, these recent examples from popular culture prompt readers and viewers to consider how cultural anxieties and norms have changed over time.

While our current century provides ample opportunities to reinvent ourselves, the reality of contemporary life also pushes us to quickly adapt to new roles and rapidly advancing computer and communication technologies. This results in the creation of a sense of tension between these new freedoms and the demands placed on us by such recent technology. One place where this tension gets reflected in popular culture is through depictions of the figure of the doppelganger. As Marcia Pointon notes in

Portrayal and the Search for Identity, in literature and other forms of cultural expression, "the doubling of bodies is troubling" (182). This is due, in large part, to the cultural anxieties the practice provokes. Indeed, while "the doppelgänger of fairy tale and myth" speaks to the cultural anxieties present in earlier eras, since the late 20th century, the figure has been associated with "anxiety around reproductive technologies and cloning" (Pointon 182).

In many cases, older depictions of the figure of the doppelganger, in fact, rely on a formula that positions the double as caught between nature and the supernatural. It is also true that, with respect to contemporary representations, there are numerous instances which show a pattern that highlights tensions related to technology. Nevertheless, the breadth and depth of contemporary examples examined in this book suggest that this is not always the case. Indeed, after exploring the symbolism and significance of the figure of the double, it becomes clear that portrayals of doppelgangers—and especially figures of the double that appear in the 21st century—do not always follow a strict continuum; rather, these contemporary representations oftentimes borrow from competing discourses.

Cultural Anxieties and Doppelgangers in the 21st Century

To an extent, 21st century representations of the figure of the double do reflect a set of concerns that were not present in earlier historical periods. This is due, in part, to the fact that new technologies now exist. Communications and cyber-technologies continue to change and advance—and newfound scientific discoveries take place—and many of these cutting-edge developments raise provocative ethical questions.

The same can be said for other emerging technologies. Consider the examples of gene mapping, gene editing, the various forms of reproductive technologies that exist (or are on the horizon), and newfound research in the field of creating intelligent machines. As our ability to map and manipulate genes grows more and more sophisticated, so do the ethical concerns that come along with these new abilities. A similar situation exists with respect to reproductive technologies. By the same token, as we get ever closer to creating Artificial Intelligence (AI), ethical issues abound. Thus, there becomes a tension between what these discoveries might afford us and the dangers they might very soon pose.

While there is anxiety and ambivalence surrounding newfound communication and computer technologies (which we can use to experiment with our identity, but which also place demands on us), there is also growing tension about the kinds of technology which can alter the very nature of the human. Together, these tensions push us, as a society, to reflect with uncertainty about the kind of advancements which, for example, might eventually lead to humans being augmented or AI being created, since these changes could fundamentally alter our concept of humanity. While concerns such as these frequently get discussed in academic circles, debates related to individualism and identity are also being explored in popular media through the plots of novels, television shows, and films—and many of the plot-lines that address these contemporary questions do so through the figure of the double.

To be clear, part of this book's argument rests on the fact that there has been a shift taking place since the dawn of the 21st century—and especially since the tragic events of September 11, 2001—in terms of the prevalent cultural anxieties that influence and, in turn, get reflected by, popular culture (anxieties which, consequently, become the subject of frequent public debate). While many controversies surface which center on emerging technologies, other debates get ushered in, as well, including those which reflect the paradigm shift brought about by the terror attacks of 9/11, the globalization that characterized the early years of the 21st century, and the attendant tensions these events have produced. To be sure, in the almost two decades since the turn of the 21st century, we are still living in the shadow of the events of 9/11, prompting many to characterize contemporary times as the "age of terror." Similarly, since the dawn of the 21st century, we have become an increasingly globalized society—for better and for worse.

At the same time, it is difficult to argue against the claim that a new scientific revolution is taking place in the world today. With the advent of so many new biomedical technologies, and the numerous scientific breakthroughs that they enable, there is the promise of a better quality of life for many of us living in the 21st century. However, there are a host of new ethical questions that these new discoveries bring about, as well. Therefore, while those of us living in the 21st century bear witness to the many exciting new medical, scientific, and technological advances taking place in contemporary times, we also must consider a new and different set of problems. Contemporary life is thus defined by a new dilemma: should medicine and science be governed by what we *can* do or what we *should* do?

Debates such as these are being dramatically portrayed in contemporary novels, television series, and films—oftentimes through representations of doppelgangers (or other forms of doubles). This is because the figure of the double is quite nuanced, complex, and malleable, and thus responsive to changing times and shifting cultural norms. Nonetheless, the fact also remains that the doppelganger is a literary archetype with a rich and varied history—and to understand contemporary representations, it is vital to know this history since modern-day texts that rely on the doppelganger inevitably reflect the long tradition from which the figure hails. To be sure, recent fiction, films, and television programs that utilize the figure draw on both this tradition and on formulas that have long been in place. The figure thus not only communicates contemporary fears, but it also helps us to engage in timeless existential debates. With this in mind, this book will analyze a number of 21st century texts as cases in point.

Literary Doppelgangers of the 21st Century

The concept and literary motif of the doppelganger can be traced backed well before the time Poe published his short story "William Wilson"—and even long before Shakespeare penned *A Comedy of Errors*, but the term *"Doppelgänger"* or doppelganger came about around the same time as the Gothic novel. The term is said to have first appeared in *Siebenkäs* (1796), a novel by Johann Paul Friedrich ("Jean Paul") Richter (1763–1825). A German romantic novel which was published in three volumes, *Siebenkäs* follows protagonist (and the titular character) Siebenkäs and his friend, Leibgeber, who is, in actuality, his alter ego (or doppelganger).

Richter is credited with coining the term, but the concept of the doppelganger has been in existence much longer—and it has persisted to this day as a seemingly inexhaustible motif. Indeed, since the dawn of the 21st century, there have been a number of novels published that treat the theme in new and different ways; these contemporary literary works thus use the figure of the double to interrogate current debates while also reintroducing an old motif (and timeless set of concerns) to a modern audience. Contemporary novels, including José Saramago's *The Double* (2002), Kazuo Ishiguro's *Never Let Me Go* (2005), Audrey Niffenegger's *Her Fearful Symmetry* (2009), Blake Crouch's *Dark Matter* (2016), Dexter Palmer's *Version Control* (2016), and Mur Lafferty's *Six Wakes* (2017), address the concept of doubling in ways that merge present-day concerns with age-old debates.

A literary horror novel that recalls the gothic tradition, Audrey Niffenegger's *Her Fearful Symmetry* is set near London's infamous Highgate Cemetery and concerns two generations of twins. The plot primarily focuses on the younger generation, identical twin sisters named Julia and Valentina, who move from Illinois to London after their aunt (their mother's twin sister) dies from leukemia. Part ghost story, part family melodrama, Niffenegger's novel relies upon, at the same time it plays with, literary conventions that were popular in previous eras. Her novel thus revises older formulas while using the theme of doubling to call attention to 21st century anxieties about identity and self-determination.

José Saramago's *The Double* follows protagonist Tertuliano Máximo Afonso, a divorced high school history teacher. One night, on the recommendation of a colleague, Tertuliano rents a movie and, in it, he spots an actor who appears to be the spitting image of how he looked five years ago. Tertuliano grows obsessed with learning the identity of this man and eventually goes as far as to stalk his double. As its plot and premise both suggest, Saramago's *The Double* not only contains echoes of Poe's "William Wilson," but it also shares much in common with Fyodor Dostoevsky's 1846 novella *The Double*. In the case of Saramago's *The Double*, while the plot reworks a formula seen elsewhere (and therefore borrows heavily from traditional representations of the figure), the novel nonetheless makes a nod to technology and its role, especially in the way Saramago both emphasizes and relies upon the presence of a VCR and the numerous video recorded copies of movies which serve as important plot devices—as well as catalysts in the narrative.

While both Niffenegger's *Her Fearful Symmetry* and Saramago's *The Double* treat the concept of doubling largely as a metaphor—and as a way to bring identity-related questions to light—a number of the other novels discussed in this book are works of science fiction, and thus, using that particular lens, their authors create worlds where mechanical doppelgangers (meaning robotic or AI counterparts), clones, or others forms of doubles exist as more than mere metaphors. For example, in *Never Let Me Go*, Kazuo Ishiguro imagines a dystopian society where biotechnology creates cloned human beings. Indeed, in *Never Let Me Go*, human cloning is not only possible, but it has advanced to the point where a whole new class of beings exist: clones, who have been created solely so that their organs can be harvested and provide replacement parts for others.

While Ishiguro relies on cloning to forward his narrative, both Blake Crouch (in *Dark Matter*) and Dexter Palmer (in *Version Control*) use the existence of parallel universes, another popular science fiction trope, to rationalize the existence of their protagonists' doppelgangers. Mur Lafferty, who sets her futuristic science fiction novel *Six Wakes* aboard an interstellar space craft, justifies the presence of many doppelgangers through the use of a technology which not only creates human clones, but which also allows their consciousness to be downloaded into new bodies.

As different genres of literature, these various novels all rely on the concept of doubling, but each does so in a way which fits its unique mode of storytelling. Indeed, while some of these literary works rely on the doppelganger theme in a more symbolic manner, others novels addressed here consider more literal versions of the figure. As Frank Dietz explains in his essay "Secret Sharers: The Doppelgänger Motif in Speculative Fiction" (where he discusses the concept of doubling), a key difference with respect to representations of doppelgangers in science fiction compared to more realistic fiction can be observed in the figure's treatment: "science fiction creates worlds in which the reader is invited to accept the figure of the double as literal fact" (210).

Such is, indeed, the case in *Never Let Me Go*, which, at its core, is a clone narrative and, hence, a novel about the ethics of cloning. The novel was, in fact, written in response to the successful cloning of Dolly, the sheep (in 1996, she was the first mammal successfully cloned from an adult somatic cell). In *Never Let Me Go*, the plot centers on protagonist Kathy H., a clone who now works as a "carer," providing comfort and medical assistance to other clones (whose organs are being harvested). For much of the novel, Kathy reminisces about her friends, Tommy and Ruth (who are also clones), and the time they spent together at Hailsham, an experimental boarding school, and, later, at a place she refers to as The Cottages, a residential complex where they lived. Some of Kathy's flashbacks focus on her close friend Ruth's search for her double. With her friends' help, Ruth, after hearing that a "possible" for her lives nearby, attempts to find this "possible," an older woman who resembles Ruth and thus could potentially be the woman from whom she was cloned. By including a subplot about one of the main character's search for her double, the book clearly reiterates the theme of "the search for self," a search which can so frequently be seen in storylines that feature the trend of doppelgangers. In this manner, the novel explores ethical issues while also raising questions about identity and the path toward self-discovery.

Blake Crouch's *Dark Matter* reflects many of these same themes. The novel begins with the apparent abduction of community college professor Jason Dessen. Professor Dessen, it turns out, has been transported against his will to an alternate universe and has switched places (so to speak) with a double of himself. In this parallel reality, Dessen is an internationally renowned quantum physicist who has managed to monetize his scientific discoveries. Though he is recognized for his brilliance and is financially successful in this timeline, Dessen finds he is lonely and missing his wife and son, so he attempts to find a way home. In the course of trying to return to his family, he learns that it was, in fact, his double who was responsible for separating him from his family and, in the course of the narrative, Dessen must face off against many different versions of himself to fight his way home. As the plot of the novel suggests, *Dark Matter* is fraught with concerns about both the dangers and promises of multiplicity. The plot device of parallel universes allows questions about identity, autonomy, and self-expression to be explored as the novel's protagonist navigates multiple worlds in an attempt to reunite with his wife and son.

Dexter Palmer's *Version Control* is a science fiction novel about a physicist who, along with the help of his team, creates a "causality violation device" (in essence, they have invented a time machine, but Philip Wright, who is the mastermind behind the invention, does not like it referred to in such a manner). This invention begins to change the fabric of their universe and, thus, because of its existence, readers get a glimpse into three possible realities and how situations in each alter the personalities and destinies of the novel's protagonists. As these details suggest, like *Dark Matter*, the novel relies on the existence of parallel universes to engage with questions of identity and to explore different "possible lives" (Palmer 155). This novel also, quite self-consciously, hearkens to the "fear of technological change" that has long-existed and remains pervasive even into the 21st century (Palmer 156).

Mur Lafferty's *Six Wakes* is a murder mystery which takes place on *The Dormire*, a vessel traveling through outer space. The plot centers on the ship's crew, a group of clones who are relocating themselves and their cargo (other clones who have been placed in stasis), to an extraterrestrial colony to escape Earth, which has been devastated by climate change and wars. Lafferty's novel, like *Never Let Me Go*, is a clone narrative and it focuses on the ethics of cloning, but it also addresses issues such as identity, individuality, and agency, fraught concepts with get further complicated because in *Six Wakes*, clones must also confront the latent memories of their previous incarnations. Lafferty imagines a future where technology permits "mind-mapping," so that new copies of individuals are not only genetically identical but also retain some of the memories of the experiences of the earlier cloned versions of themselves.

What they share in common is that Lafferty's *Six Wakes*, like Niffenegger's *Her Fearful Symmetry*, Saramago's *The Double*, Ishiguro's *Never Let Me Go*, Crouch's *Dark Matter*, and Palmer's *Version Control*, all represent the figure of the double in a manner that addresses contemporary debates alongside age-old questions. By relying on traditional formulas, but altering (and sometimes subverting) them to a degree, these works of 21st century fiction reveal the malleability and durability of the doppelganger. They also showcase the tension between what contemporary discoveries—whether scientific, medical, or technological—can offer us and the dangers they might soon pose. Indeed, reading about these fictional scenarios functions, also, as a way to process real-world tensions related to emerging technologies.

Doppelgangers in 21st Century Television and Film

Similarly, watching scenarios dramatically play out on screen offers 21st century audiences a way to come to terms with the many cultural anxieties that new technologies provoke. To be sure, within both contemporary television and film, there are many examples which rely upon the figure of the doppelganger to reflect these cultural tensions. For instance, television programs, such as *The Lying Game* (2011–2013), *Ringer* (2011–2012), *Fringe* (2008–2013), *Battlestar Galactica* (2004–2009), *Orphan Black* (2013–2017), and *Westworld* (2016–present), all represent the figure of the double in ways that borrow from established formulas, but also push the boundaries through depictions of doppelgangers that call attention to 21st century debates. In the television series *Ringer* and *The Lying Game*, representations hearken back to dramatic models that were popular in the 20th century, but they also raise new questions by engaging with recent controversies.

So, while television shows including *Fringe*, *Battlestar Galactica*, *Orphan Black*, and *Westworld* contain echoes of earlier narrative traditions, they depend strongly, as well, on plot devices made popular by 21st century science fiction, such as those related to Artificial Intelligence (AI), cloning, and parallel universes. Similar scenarios also appear in recent science fiction films, such as *The Island* (2005), *The Prestige* (2006), and *Oblivion* (2013), all of which push audiences to view the double amidst 21st century debates related to ethics and identity. These films, of course, also rely upon the figure of the double to address contemporary anxieties related to emerging technologies.

A television drama that re-imagines and offers an update of the twin formula (a formula that was quite popular in the 20th century) is ABC Family's *The Lying Game*, a show which debuted in 2011. The series centers on Emma Becker (played by Alexandra Chando). Emma is a good-natured teenager who had been living with a foster family until she discovers that she has an identical twin sister named Sutton Mercer (also played by Alexandra Chando). The girls were separated at birth, with Sutton being adopted by wealthy parents and living a seemingly perfect life. Sutton convinces Emma to step into her life for a few days so she can learn about their birth mother in Los Angeles. Days turn into many weeks and both girls find themselves encountering mishaps as they try to assume the other's identity.

Starring Sarah Michelle Gellar who plays a set of identical twin sisters, *Ringer* is an American television series that premiered on The CW Network in 2011. *Ringer*, like *The Lying Game*, offers an update on the twin formula by following twin sisters Bridget Kelly and Siobhan Martin. One twin, Bridget Kelly, is a recovering drug addict who makes a living as an exotic dancer in Wyoming, while the other is an affluent Manhattan housewife. The series begins with Bridget fleeing to New York to get away from her employer, an organized crime boss named Bodaway Macawi (Zahn McClarnon), whom she witnessed commit murder. Once in New York, Bridget meets up with her estranged twin sister, Siobhan Martin, but, soon after Bridget arrives in New York, Siobhan, who had kept her twin's existence secret from her husband and friends, mysteriously disappears when the two go out on a boat. After Siobhan's apparent suicide, Bridget assumes her sister's identity and tries to fit in among Siobhan's affluent Manhattan social circle.

Fringe, an American science fiction television series created by J.J. Abrams, Alex Kurtzman, and Roberto Orci, premiered in the United States in 2008 on the Fox television network. *Fringe* engages with the motif of the double by using the plot device of parallel universes. The show follows a Federal Bureau of Investigation "Fringe Division" team, which uses unconventional "fringe" science and FBI investigative techniques to get to the bottom of a series of strange occurrences which are related to mysteries surrounding the parallel universe. Rather than featuring twins, in *Fringe* there are two identical looking women who are instead doppelgangers, hailing from parallel universes. The women (both played by Anna Torv) share the same name and face and are both special agents with the Fringe Division, but the two possess different personality traits and have had divergent lives.

Battlestar Galactica (also referred to as *BSG*) is an American science fiction television series, and part of the *Battlestar Galactica* franchise. The show was developed by Ronald D. Moore as a reimagining of the 1978 *Battlestar Galactica* television series created by Glen A. Larson. The television series first aired as a three-hour miniseries in 2003 on the Sci-Fi Channel. In *BSG*, multiplicity is made manifest through the plot device of numerous human-looking "Cylon" models ("Cylon" stands for Cybernetic Life Form Nodule), a race of sentient machines. As beings, these Cylons raise provocative ontological questions because in addition to re-imagines the formula of the doppelganger, the series also relies on these Cylons to complicate, if not altogether dissolve, binaries such as human/machine, thinking/programming, and natural/artificial.

Westworld is an American science fiction television series created by Jonathan Nolan and Lisa Joy. The television series debuted in 2016 on HBO and is based on the 1973 film of the same name (the film was written and directed by Michael Crichton). Though as a whole, the series' primary focus is related to the creation of sentient artificial intelligence, *Westworld* also includes treatment of the doppelganger motif through the character of Bernard Lowe (a sentient AI), who is an exact replica of a (now-deceased) human male named Arnold Weber (both Bernard Lowe and Arnold Weber—who appears in the series via a photograph and multiple flashbacks—are played by actor Jeffrey Wright). Bernard, who for a time remains unaware of both the fact that he is an AI and a copy of another person, works as the head of the Delos Corporation's Westworld Programming Division. Through the character of Bernard, the show engages with current debates about ethics and technology while also revisiting age-old concerns about identity, agency, and autonomy.

The Canadian science fiction television series *Orphan Black*, which debuted in the U.S. on BBC America in 2013, reworks the doppelganger motif through the existence of multiple clones (and hence is another example of a clone narrative). The series stars Tatiana Maslany who plays Sarah Manning and several of her fellow clones—all of whom are genetically identically and were born by in vitro fertilization (and are part of a project code-named Leda). Through the various characters Maslany portrays, as well as through many of the episodes' plot-lines, the series revisits the age-old debate of nature versus nurture while also raising provocative and timely questions about agency, identity, and human rights in the 21st century.

The Island, directed by Michael Bay, is a 2005 movie that follows Lincoln Six Echo (played by Ewan McGregor) and Jordan Two Delta (played by Scarlett Johannsson). The two, along with a group of other apparent survivors, reside in an elaborate underground bunker. They have been conditioned to believe that there has been a recent environmental disaster on Earth that makes most of the land uninhabitable. They, along with the other supposed survivors, are waiting to win a "lottery" which will send them to an island paradise far away from their current dwelling. When Jordan Two Delta wins this (so-called) lottery, Lincoln Six Echo stumbles upon the horrific truth: they are actually clones, generated to provide replacement organs to the owners of insurance policies. Not only does *The Island* work as a cautionary tale about the perils of scientific advancement, it also brings up issues related to agency, individualism, and human rights.

The Prestige, a 2006 film directed by Christopher Nolan, features two sets of doubles. The film actually relies upon both twins and clones as part of its plot, which centers on the competition between rival magicians, Robert Angier (played by Hugh Jackman) and Alfred Borden (played by Christian Bale), who vie to see which of them can create the most compelling stage illusion. Once friends and colleagues, a vicious rivalry between the two magicians begins when one accidentally kills the other's wife as part of a stage act by tying a trick knot incorrectly. Both men ultimately perform a variation of an act called the "Transported Man," where each illusionist seems to instantly travel between two spots on stage. The magicians pull off this trick because, in one case, there are actually two men—identical twin brothers (played by Bale)—who pretend to be the same person, and in the other case, the performer creates and then kills clones of himself with the help of a duplicating machine, which was created by Nikola Tesla. Thus, as these details of the film's plot suggest, *The Prestige* revisits the twin formula while also addressing the role of technology.

Oblivion is a 2013 science fiction film based on Joseph Kosinski's graphic novel of the same name (Kosinski also directed the film). The film follows Jack Harper (played by Tom Cruise), a tech repairman who lives in close orbit to a post-apocalyptic Earth. Jack has been conditioned to believe that he is one of a small number of human survivors and that once he finishes his job, he can join the others on Titan, which is now the site of a human colony. Jack, however, grows suspicious of the story he has been fed due to latent memories that have been resurfacing; this, combined with some startling discoveries he makes, leads him to eventually learn the truth: he is one of many clones who have been created by hostile aliens who need help with clean-up on Earth. Like so many of the other storylines that involve doubles, *Oblivion* deals with subjects such as memory, agency, and identity, but, to forward its plot, the film also relies on cutting-edge technology—in this case, extra-terrestrial technology—thus bringing its role into debate, as well.

Recent Trends

What these varied and numerous cases make clear is that storylines featuring doubles (whether twins, clones, or doppelgangers) have been quite popular in recent years. These many examples share in common the fact that they showcase our cultural fixation with issues related to autonomy and human rights. These contemporary examples also raise provocative questions about individuality and agency—and they push the boundaries about what these issues mean to a 21st century audience. To address these concerns, this project offers close analysis of these various texts, which together reflect a range of 21st century novels, television shows, and films. Divided into two sections, this book examines how the figure of the double functions in these various forms of popular culture.

Section I, "Literature," offers literary analysis of six contemporary novels—specifically, Audrey Niffenegger's *Her Fearful Symmetry*, José Saramago's *The Double*, Kazuo Ishiguro's *Never Let Me Go*, Blake Crouch's *Dark Matter*, Dexter Palmer's *Version Control*, and Mur Lafferty's *Six Wakes*—and explores how these works treat the literary motif of the doppelganger. As part of this project, these chapters consider how 21st century literary doppelgangers rely upon the long literary tradition of featuring various forms of doubles and they also address how the figure's significance has taken on new meaning in recent years.

Section II, "Television and Film," discusses recent television shows—these include *Westworld, Orphan Black, Fringe, Battlestar Galactica, The Lying Game*, and *Ringer*—as well as contemporary films, such as *The Island, The Prestige*, and *Oblivion*, with an eye toward addressing how the figure of the double functions in these recent cultural products. This book makes connections between points raised in the two sections and it also focuses on how different forms of media and popular culture treat the durable figure of the double. The book's chapters also consider the texts analyzed in the context of questions such as genre, history, and audience.

Section I.
Literature

"I am the enemy within. I am the boss of your dreams. See. Your hand shakes. It is not palsy or booze. It is your Doppelgänger trying to get out. Beware."
—Anne Sexton, "Rumpelstiltskin"

In her poem "Rumpelstiltskin," Anne Sexton (1928–1974) offers an interesting retelling of the notorious imp, by re-imagining him as a doppelganger hiding within, waiting to get out. The fact that Sexton chooses to envision Rumpelstiltskin in this manner is remarkable, not least of all because the story of Rumpelstiltskin—albeit under a different name—is believed to be around 4000 years old. The fact that this story has survived for millennia suggests that it speaks to timeless concerns.

Like Rumpelstiltskin, the figure of the doppelganger has also been around for millennia, and it has appeared in literature in many different forms and in various plots. It, too, has existed as a perennial image—and, it, too, remains popular still today because of the timeless set of concerns it provokes. A literary archetype, the doppelganger has been traditionally imagined in the form of an identical twin or some other type of look-a-like. In most cases, however, literary doppelgangers have gone much further than being mere look-a-likes since the resemblance they share tends to go beyond the physical. As Tony Fonseca points out in "The Doppelgänger," the figure is often related to literary motifs such as "the evil twin" and "the alter ego," both of which are subsets of the doppelganger (188). Building upon these descriptions, Joanne Blum emphasizes in *Transcending Gender: The Male/Female Double in Women's Fiction* that the doppelganger usually represents a fragmentation of self into dual or even multiple personalities, thereby further suggesting a psychological component. To be sure, this quality is a hallmark feature of the double, going back to its earliest iterations—and, indeed, this concept of the double gets reflected in more recent literary works like Sexton's poem, where she pictures Rumpelstiltskin as a doppelganger that emerges from within.

The Literary Motif

An old motif, the doppelganger still remains both popular and relevant today. Indeed, while it is true that as long as there have been stories, various forms of doubles have existed, the figure, rather than going out of fashion, has proven to be malleable as well as inexhaustible. However, as David J. Burrows emphasizes in *Myths and Motifs in Literature*, "the use of the double has changed in literary treatment throughout the centuries" (382). Indeed, by surveying representations from earlier historical periods, it is possible to trace the different ways the figure has traditionally been deployed in literary works:

> During the medieval period, component aspects of a single human being might be objectified as separate people, as the body and the soul were in the medieval debate. Later, the contending forces of good and evil within the individual were objectified as figures such as the good and bad angels in Christopher Marlowe's *Dr. Faustus*. Still later, authors were to create characters who were representative parts of aspects of but a single individual [Burrows 382].

Though depictions of the motif have shifted over time, there are pervasive traits associated with the figure. The double represents the "construction of self-identity," yet also "emerges as the other that literature has to grapple with," according to Dimitris Vardoulakis, who writes about the doppelganger in his book *The Doppelgänger: Literature's Philosophy* (xiii). In the words of Susan Yi Sencindiver, who discusses the recurring literary device of the doppelganger in her essay "Sexing or Specularising the Doppelgänger," the figure also "articulates the disturbing crisis of self-division and identity as alterity" (64).

As these remarks by Burrows, Vardoulakis, and Sencindiver make clear, there is much currency bound up with the figure, which has proven to be an enduring literary motif. Indeed, beyond Shakespeare, Poe, Dostoevsky, and Sexton, all of whom relied on either twins or other forms of doubles in their literary works, other notable authors such as Elizabeth Gaskell (1810–1865), Charles Dickens (1812–1870), Henry James (1843–1916), Joseph Conrad (1857–1924), and Vladimir Nabokov (1899–1977), among many others, have relied on this formula, as well.

Whether confronting a ghastly likeness of oneself, which is what happens to the character Lucy in Gaskell's novella *The Poor Clare* (1856), or meeting a stranger with whom one shares an uncanny resemblance, which is what Sydney Carton is faced with in Dickens' *A Tale of Two Cities* (1859) and also what happens to the captain who saves a stranger from drowning in Conrad's story "The Secret Sharer" (1909), to being haunted by one's alter ego, which Spencer Brydon encounters in James's "The Jolly Corner" (1908), 19th and early 20th century fiction is replete with examples of characters who must confront their shadow side when they come face-to-face with their doppelganger.

Writers continued this pattern well into the 20th century, sometimes offering a new spin on an old idea. For instance, in the case of Nabokov's novel *Despair* (1934), the twist is that readers are left wondering whether the likeness between two strangers who are apparent doubles may not be actual but could likely exist, instead, only in the mind only of one of the two men. As these many examples make clear, there are abundant cases of doppelgangers in literary works.

What, then, accounts for the fact that this figure—in its various forms—consistently appears and reappears in stories? What does it suggest—and why does it matter—that the trope can be found in stories from different cultures and across historical periods? To be sure, the reappearance of the figure suggests that the literary archetype is both timeless and malleable and, hence, able to adapt in response to changing times, shifting social norms, and competing cultural anxieties. As John Yorke emphasizes in an article he wrote for the *Atlantic Monthly*, "storytelling is an indispensable human preoccupation, as important to us all—almost—as breathing" and, consequently, "it behooves us then to try and understand it." It is also true that when a motif recurs in literature to the degree that the double does, it is incumbent upon us to try to decipher its importance.

The literary figure of the doppelganger has proven to be both a resilient and inexhaustible device. It has appeared in different forms over time because its meaning has changed in response to cultural factors. Consequently, exploring how cultural anxieties get projected onto (at the same time as they are echoed by) the figure of the doppelganger communicates much to us about different cultures as well as about the nature of storytelling—and its profound effect on humans across time.

As Milica Zivkovic points out in the article "The Double as the 'Unseen' of Culture: Toward a Definition of Doppelgänger," the doppelganger figure exists as a cultural construction and thus appears in the mythology, legends, and religion of particular cultures. However, while the figure has persisted as a perennial motif and is present in a range of literary styles, periods, and genres, the doppelganger is neither "free," nor does it exist outside time but, rather, gets produced within, and is determined by, its social context (Zivkovic).

Literary Doubles in Contemporary Times

Even into the 21st century, the figure of the double continues to appear in various forms. In the case of contemporary novels, sometimes plot developments rely on rather traditional depictions of doppelgangers. In other instances, however, doubles exist as a result of emerging (or even science fictional) technology; these cases thus reflect recent scientific and technological breakthroughs and the promise as well as anxiety that come along with them.

Yet, in all of the cases examined in this section, the inclusion of the doppelganger motif raises interesting questions about the nature of identity. Chapter 1, which is entitled "Twinning in Audrey Niffenegger's *Her Fearful Symmetry*," surveys a novel which offers a 21st century reimagining of a plot pattern that was common in previous eras: the family melodrama. Niffenegger's novel, which recalls the gothic tradition (even to the point that she includes a ghost story!), borrows, blurs, and blends a number of literary conventions that were popular in centuries past. Her novel thus revises older formulas while treating the theme of twins in a manner that also calls to mind contemporary cultural anxieties. This book's second chapter, "The Pursuit of Self? José Saramago's *The Double*," addresses the concept of individualism and also discusses how Saramago updates a classic representation of the doppelganger figure, one that echoes earlier literary accounts.

The book's third chapter, "The Ethics of Cloning in Kazuo Ishiguro's *Never Let Me Go*," looks at the treatment of the themes of identity and autonomy while also discussing how Ishiguro's novel serves as a warning about the ethical dilemmas that cloning human beings will inevitably bring about. Chapter 4, "Through a Machine Darkly: Blake Crouch's *Dark Matter*," shows a man forced to confront his shadow side by making him face off against of series of doppelgangers, all of whom are intent on the same thing. As part of its treatment of the concept of doubling, *Dark Matter* also brings to the forefront questions about the role environment and experiences play in shaping identity and Crouch relies upon another popular science fiction trope, the multiverse theory (which posits the existence of parallel universes), to explore these concerns.

Like Crouch's *Dark Matter*, Dexter Palmer's *Version Control* uses parallel universes to consider identity-related concerns. This subject, as well as his treatment of the literary doppelganger, is the focus of Chapter 5, "Technology and the Self in Dexter Palmer's *Version Control*." The last chapter in this section, "Clones (and Crime) in Space: Mur Lafferty's *Six Wakes*," considers both the issue of autonomy and the ethics of cloning, but complicates these debates by having clones retain the memories of their previous incarnations; because of this detail, the novel thus considers the relationship between memory and identity. *Six Wakes* also raises provocative questions about the ethics of immortality (since clones' consciousness could conceivably live forever).

All of these novels push readers to contemplate the nature of identity while, at the same time, they showcase timely debates about individualism, autonomy, agency, and human rights. Many of the storylines involving doubles also reflect the adage "you are your own worst enemy." In several cases, literary treatments of the double call attention to the anxiety that has long-been associated with the figure of the double. Moreover, these stories frequently hint at what underpins this anxiety by suggesting that both fear of self and fear of death are at its root.

1. Twinning in Audrey Niffenegger's *Her Fearful Symmetry*

American author Audrey Niffenegger (born in 1963) remains best known for her commercially successful debut, *The Time Traveler's Wife* (2003), a novel which was later turned into a film directed by Robert Schwentke and starring A-list actors Eric Bana and Rachel McAdams (while the reviews were mixed, the film adaptation was a financial success). Niffenegger's 2009 novel, *Her Fearful Symmetry*, however, has also proven to be an important cultural text for the way it treats the concept of doubling by reimagining the twin formula. Although the narrative's treatment of the double calls attention to anxieties that have long-been associated with the figure—such as fear of self and fear of death—as a 21st century text, this novel also engages with contemporary debates related to the changing nature of identity in a postmodern world.

A literary horror novel written in the gothic tradition, Niffenegger's *Her Fearful Symmetry* takes place in London, right beside the city's infamous Highgate Cemetery, and its complicated plot centers on two generations of twins. The younger generation consists of twenty-year-old identical twin sisters named Julia and Valentina. The girls have recently moved from Illinois to London. Their aunt Elspeth (their mother's twin sister), who has recently passed away after battling leukemia, has left them her London flat and the girls decide to take up residence there. Elspeth's ghost, it turns out, is trapped in the apartment with them, and the girls eventually become aware of her presence. As the months pass, it becomes clear that Valentina, in particular, has a connection with Elspeth, and the two learn to communicate with one another. Also, as time goes by, the family's secrets come to light.

A narrative that blends a ghost story with a family melodrama, this novel relies upon, at the same time it plays with, literary conventions that were popular in earlier eras. In particular, Niffenegger uses traits commonly found in the Gothic mode. In this manner, Niffenegger's novel thus revises older formulas while relying on the ever-popular theme of doubling to call attention to 21st century anxieties about identity, individualism, and self-determination.

The Twin Formula

The novel makes it clear that, throughout their lives, twin sisters Julia and Valentina have been inseparable. The twins are identical in appearance—mirror images, in fact—but there are nonetheless differences between the sisters. Julia has always been the dominant twin, a feature which manifests both in her personality and in her physiology since she is outgoing and healthy while Valentina, the more demure of the two, suffers from asthma and has a heart valve that never been properly formed (she is sometimes ill as a result of this). While Julia comes across as stronger, both physically and emotionally, Valentina is the more intuitive of the two, a trait which allows her to sense, and ultimately communicate with, Elspeth's ghost.

A recurring source of tension throughout the narrative concerns the fact that Valentina feels conflicted about being a twin. She worries that she does not have her own identity and that rather, she exists merely as half of a whole. She is especially anxious about being the weaker twin, both physically and emotionally, a difference which Julia is also well aware of (and one she, at times, exploits and calls attention to). Valentina eventually grows more resilient and eventually decides that she must break away from Julia in order to establish her own identity.

Together with Elspeth's help, Valentina hatches a strange plan to, in effect, use death to separate herself from her sister. She persuades Elspeth to take out her soul (a move Elspeth accidentally performed on an unwitting kitten) as a way to convince everyone that she has died. The idea is that she will, in effect, fake her own death, only to come back free to live her life without Julia (since Julia will assume she is dead). Elspeth and Valentina eventually carry out this plan and stage it to look like Valentina dies of an asthma attack. When Julia discovers her sister's lifeless body, she is overcome with grief. Elspeth later gives Valentina the opportunity to re-enter her body, but she refuses, so Elspeth decides to take over her body.

While this bizarre plot strand is playing out, the family's long-buried secrets are also being unearthed. The diaries and letters that Elspeth left behind when she died reveal a startling discovery: years ago, Edie and Elspeth switched places. The woman everyone knows to be Elspeth is, in fact, Edie—and the woman everyone assumes to be Edie is actually Elspeth. The real Edie is the mother of Julia and Valentina.

The reason for this switch traces back to an encounter which took place before Julia and Valentina's birth. Elspeth had been engaged to marry an American man named Jack, who was living and working in London, but she was insecure in their relationship. To test Jack, she posed as Edie and made sexual advances toward him. However, one night, after a party, Jack and the actual Edie slept together. As a result of their tryst, Edie (who was pretending to be Elspeth) became pregnant with the twins. For his part, Jack did not realize that he had slept with Edie because he was too drunk to remember it. Elspeth, however, learns what happens. While she goes through with marrying Jack, it is her sister Edie who moves to the United States with him, and, once there, she gives birth to twin daughters, Julia and Valentina. Edie brings them to London while they are still babies, and Elspeth and Edie decide to switch places.

As these plot details suggest, Niffenegger relies on a number of tropes common to twin narratives. Between the girls' fears of sameness, to storylines about twins switching places and role reversals, and on to cases of mistaken identity, Niffenegger revisits many of the patterns common to twin tales. In fact, Juliana de Nooy discusses many of these same patterns in her book-length study, *Twins in Contemporary Literature and Culture: Look Twice*.

In this book, de Nooy emphasizes, as part of her discussion of literary representations of twins, how "textual twins," as she refers to them, often suffer "pitfalls of stagnation," wherein the uniqueness of the two individuals collapse into one identity (45). The situation de Nooy describes here relates to the conundrum that the first generation twins, Elspeth and Edie, faced, since the two prove to be virtually indistinguishable from each other. This results in identity confusion, a consequence which is far from uncommon. Indeed, oftentimes when twins, especially twin girls, appear in literary texts, once there is a case of "mistaken identity," their individual identities are never "fully restored," rather "their lives intersect in unpredictable ways" (de Nooy 162). The dilemma that de Nooy refers to here is also the very one that causes such anxiety in the novel for young Valentina, a girl who fears that her identity has been overshadowed by her more dominant twin sister's persona.

In the case of Valentina, this fear pushes her headlong toward her own death, which symbolically works to show the destructive possibilities bound together with the search for self and identity. Moreover, because part of the plot of *Her Fearful Symmetry* rests on the young woman hatching a plan where she will pretend to die, the novel displays another pattern common to twin narratives: the plot device of a twin faking her own death. Linda Ruth Williams, in her book *The Erotic Thriller in Contemporary Cinema*, describes the prevalence of this trope, suggesting that the use of a twin's "(faked) death" functions as a way to have the other twin "question her own identity" (Williams 32).

Beyond the many traits described above, the novel also demonstrates an adherence to what is commonly referred to as the "good twin/bad twin" formula, a pattern characterized by positioning a naïve young woman against her more experienced twin sister. Symbolically, this formula works to "represent conflicting desires and attitudes" (de Nooy 163). Moreover, the "'good twin/bad twin' premise" often works to highlights stereotypes about females, by painting the good twin as virtuous (sometimes even "frigid") while portraying the bad twin as "promiscuous" (Williams 355).

Niffenegger's Reliance on the Gothic Tradition

While Niffenegger weaves her narrative about twin sisters Julia and Valentina, and as she reveals details about their family's secrets, it becomes clear that she is relying on traits commonly found not only in twin narratives, but also those made popular by the Gothic mode to bring the novel's concerns to bear. Certainly, the plot, characters, and (especially) mysteries at the heart of her novel *Her Fearful Symmetry* call to mind the Gothic literary tradition, a mode which began in the mid–18th century in Europe and flourished into the 19th century (scholars generally agree that the first major Gothic novel was Horace Walpole's *The Castle of Otranto*, which was published in 1764).

The "Gothic is marked by an anxious encounter with otherness, with the dark and mysterious unknown," a point that Ruth Bienstock Anolik notes in the Introduction to *The Gothic Other: Racial and Social Constructions in the Literary Imagination* (1). In "Double Trouble," Carolyn Banks succinctly summarizes the tell-tale signs of the Gothic mode. She notes that these include "the creepy old mansion and the brooding minor characters and the hideous, slowly unraveling family secrets" (Banks).

As Julian Wolfreys describes it in his book *Victorian Hauntings: Spectrality, Gothic, the Uncanny and Literature*, there existed a Gothic sensibility that was quite prevalent in the 19th century. This sensibility was characterized by hauntings and other forays into the realm of the supernatural. As Wolfreys defines it, the Gothic tradition reflected "the increasingly ghost-ridden world of the nineteenth century" (83). He further contends that the "Victorian frame of mind" (as he puts it) is, in literature, so frequently "translated into a haunted house" (83). Yet, as part of its formulation, this literary mode seeks to unsettle and call into question accepted modes of knowledge. Hence, "the effect of the Gothic [...] is to destabilize discourses of power and knowledge" (Wolfreys 11).

Thus, as a literary mode, the Gothic has proven quite useful. Indeed, "from its early manifestations in the turbulent eighteenth century, this seemingly escapist mode has provided a useful ground upon which to safely confront very real fears and horrors" (Anolik 1). Although many of the conceits typical to Gothic literature come across as fanciful and even superficial, this dimension of the mode allows it to bring cultural anxieties to the forefront. In fact, in "The Woman at the Window," Marilyn Butler goes as far as to argue that the same qualities that categorize the Gothic mode as mere escapism actually open up a space to explore very real fears.

To be sure, these same qualities that made the Gothic mode popular in centuries past also make the tradition ripe for imitation and borrowing by contemporary authors. Indeed, just as Banks notes, there is a tendency of contemporary writers of commercial fiction to play "with the Gothic tradition." Such is the case in Niffenegger's novel, *Her Fearful Symmetry*, where she relies on the proximity of a cemetery (and the sense of spectral haunting that goes along with it), the presence of multiple ghosts, cases of mistaken identity, and long-buried family secrets to propel her narrative about twins.

A Trick Found in Shakespeare and in Soap Operas

For a novel that bears the signs of so much influence of the Gothic tradition, it may seem surprising that Niffenegger also relies on a plot device found in several of William Shakespeare's plays: the "bed switch trick." However, there is a connection between these two (seemingly distinct) literary traditions. Shakespeare has, in fact, long been credited as inspiring the Gothic mode. Indeed, according to Tabish Khair, who makes this claim in *The Gothic, Postcolonialism, and Otherness: Ghosts from Elsewhere*, Shakespeare was a "major influence on Gothic Literature" (Khair 7). Shakespeare relied on ghosts in a number of his plays (most notably, perhaps, in the tragedies, *Hamlet* and *Macbeth*) and he, of course, also time after time, relied upon the motif of twins and doubling in his plays.

Yet, Shakespeare also used a device known as the "bed switch trick" (sometime referred to as a "bed trick") in several of his plays including *Measure for Measure, All's Well that Ends Well*, and *The Two Noble Kinsmen*. In Shakespeare's plays, the maneuver appears as it traditionally does in literature: a man thinks he is going to have sexual relations with a certain woman, and without his knowledge, that woman's place is taken by a substitute. In essence, the "bed trick" deceives a would-be-lover into sleeping with a person who is pretending to be someone else. This guise works not only as part of the plot, but also as a key to the resolution of Shakespeare's (so-called) problem play, *All's Well that Ends Well* (1604). Helena for so long has pined after Bertram—she loves him and wishes to marry him—but Bertram, believing that he is above her in station, staunchly refuses. When Helena cures the Duke (who is suffering from a fistula), the Duke, in appreciation, tells her that he will allow her to wed whomever she chooses. She, of course, selects Bertram as her groom-to-be, but he still rejects her, saying that he will only marry her after she wears his ring and is pregnant with his child—a set of circumstances he intends to avoid (so, he in effect makes what he believes to be an idle promise).

Meanwhile, Bertram is trying seduce another young woman named Maria. Maria is not interested, but Bertram is not really taking "no" for an answer. Consequently, the two women come up with a plan. Maria accepts Bertram's ring (which he has offered to her in an attempt to seduce her) and tells him she will meet him late at night for a liaison. Instead, Bertram finds Helena waiting for him, yet he does not realize that it is her because of the dark of night. She gets possession of his ring and also gets pregnant as a result of their encounter—in other words, the "bed switch trick" succeeds. Recall that a scenario quite similar to this occurs in *Her Fearful Symmetry* since Jack is deceived into sleeping with (and impregnating) Edie because he is drunk and believes her to be Elspeth—and, in fact, similar situations can also be found in the storylines of many 20th and 21st century soap operas (indeed, the popular television series *Once Upon a Time* and *Passions* both include treatment of the "bed switch trick"). Significantly, at their core, both story-lines about twins and plots that include "bed switching" (a trick which relies upon mistaken identity) both relate to concerns about identity and individualism.

To be sure, both tropes also speak to the tensions that questions about identity and the self inevitably bring about. The fact that doubling and mistaken identity figured into so many of Shakespeare's plays and that, hundreds of years later, these concerns continue to emerge and re-emerge—in Gothic literature, in various literary modes made popular in the 20th century, and even into the 21st century—suggest their perennial nature. Moreover, their continued reappearance also suggests a degree of malleability with respect to what they can represent to a given culture. Indeed, various forms of doubles—including twins—continually reemerge precisely because of their ability to hearken to age-old debates while also addressing contemporary concerns

Tensions about Twins in the 21st Century

In her article "The Power of Two: Twins in Literature," Ann Morgan assesses the popularity and widespread appeal of novels about twins. She explains that these narratives "are intriguing because they allow the exploration of what might have been. By running two lives that started from the same point off along divergent tracks, they throw up questions about our uniqueness, and the chances and choices that make us who we are" (Morgan). Indeed, identity-related questions such as the ones Morgan alludes to get dramatically played out in story-lines about twins—and this has long been their appeal. In the 21st century, these same concerns, of course, still persist; yet, in contemporary times, these age-old questions appear alongside newer ones.

Clearly, part of this new permutation of the long-pervasive trend of representing twins in literature has to do with the fact that we now have more and more ways to try on new identities. To be sure, in the 21st century, narratives about twins remind us of the many (potentially divergent) paths we have to choose from, a reality only heightened by the advent of new technologies which provide ample opportunities for frequent self-expression—and even reinvention. Because of the many available social and professional networking sites (not to mention the numerous gaming servers out there), all of which grant us the freedom to actively construct an identity (or even different identities), we now have the ability to self-fashion, in other words, we can consciously create our identity and public persona in any way we choose. These new choices offer much promise, but they can be overwhelming, too—and, thus, the source of much anxiety.

Twin narratives, therefore, call attention to these new ways we can communicate and self-construct in the 21st century. At the same time, though, narratives about twins also bring to mind the changes brought about by new reproductive technologies. These cutting-edge breakthroughs in reproductive medicine promise much (they bring hope to infertile couples and have the potential to effect other medical advances), but they also can be seen as threatening since some people fear that science may be taken too far. Hence, there is a cultural ambivalence which exists surrounding these discoveries.

Further adding to the public's awareness of these new discoveries in reproductive technology, there has been a palpable increase in the number of twins born in recent decades. Indeed, thanks to a phenomenon that many refer to as the "IVF-effect," there are actually many more twins nowadays than there ever have been before. Writing in April of 2014 for the *Atlantic Monthly*, Alexis C. Madrigal explains that there are about a million so-called "extra" twins, the result of the many assistive reproductive technologies (ART) now available. Indeed, the prevalence of the use of reproductive technology to treat infertility through procedures such as *in vitro* fertilization make twins more and more common. Though promising, the advent of these new forms of medical technology also raise questions about bioethics—and are thus a cause of societal tension.

As a 21st century text, Audrey Niffenegger's novel, *Her Fearful Symmetry*, exists in the midst of these many debates that are being brought about by the various technological changes taking place today. To be sure, her novel represents twins in ways that merge contemporary controversies with long-standing questions. In this manner, her reliance on older formulas and traditions work to hearken to both traditional concerns—such as those related to identity and autonomy—while also reflecting current cultural anxieties about the nature of individualism in the 21st century.

2. The Pursuit of Self? José Saramago's *The Double*

"In a dark time, the eye begins to see, I meet my shadow in the deepening shade."—Theodore Roethke, "In a Dark Time"

"In a Dark Time" is one of the most personal and harrowing poems written by American writer Theodore Roethke (1908–1963). The confessional poem begins with a violent description of a psychic breakdown, a reference to Roethke's own mental illness, which he credits as the source of his troubles as well as his inspiration. In this poem, however, Roethke also speaks of the search for self and references his shadow side, thus invoking the literary motif of the double and its traditional symbolism.

In a manner that hearkens back to the way Roethke addresses this set of concerns in his poem, in his 2002 novel, *The Double*, Portuguese born author José Saramago (1922–2010) similarly uses the lens of literature to discuss mental illness alongside his literary treatment of the motif of the double. Indeed, at its core, *The Double* is a novel about a man's descent into madness after learning about the existence of his doppelganger, a person who represents his shadow side.

While Nobel Prize winning author José de Sousa Saramago was a novelist, playwright, and journalist who, over the course of his career, wrote in a variety of genres, he remains best known for his novels that blend "surrealist experimentation with a kind of sardonic peasant pragmatism" (Eberstadt). One such novel is *The Double*, which, as its title implies, offers a new spin on the literary archetype of the doppelganger. In *The Double*, there are signposts—such as details about technology and the other minutia of contemporary life—that suggest when this story takes place, but Saramago's novel is largely devoid of details about its geographic setting. As Gerald T. Cobb explains in "A Dilemma of Identity," instead of "conventional descriptions of locale or setting, Saramago offers minute philosophical descriptions of the transactions of everyday life." An effect of this is that the symbolism of the story overshadows any regional or national focus, making the novel come across instead as an anthem for contemporary times rather than a novel about place.

The Doppelganger Motif

The Double concerns a protagonist named Tertuliano Máximo Afonso, a divorced high school teacher who plunges headlong into obsession after watching a movie recommended to him by a colleague. In that movie, he catches sight of a bit-part actor with whom he bears an uncanny physical resemblance. While there appears, at first, to be subtle differences between the two men, Tertuliano soon realizes that this man looks exactly the same as how he looked five years ago. He also soon discovers that the film is actually several years old, which pushes him to correctly conjecture that he and this mysterious man are, in fact, the same age and identical in appearance to one another.

The fact that there is a man out there who looks exactly like him is too much for Tertuliano to bear. He cannot get the image of his double out of his mind, which leads to him becoming obsessed with learning the identity of this man—and ultimately pushes him to the brink of madness. Indeed, Tertuliano eventually goes as far as to stalk his double, a man named António Claro. The men then become embroiled in a dark game with each other, one which involves deceiving the women in their lives—and which ultimately costs António Claro his life and leaves Tertuliano with an uncertain fate.

As both its plot and premise suggest, Saramago's novel not only hearkens back to Poe's story "William Wilson" (notably, both literary works concern doubles who share a birthday—and both end tragically), but it also has traits in common with Fyodor Dostoevsky's 1846 novella *The Double* (particularly with respect to theme and plot similarities). Although Saramago's *The Double* reworks a formula seen in other well-known literary works, and though it also clearly borrows from traditional representations of the figure of the literary doppelganger, the novel departs from these representations, as well.

Specifically, the role played by technology—particularly the way Saramago relies upon a VCR and numerous video recorded copies of movies, all of which serve as important plot devices—sets *The Double* apart from some of its literary predecessors. In this regard, Saramago represents the doppelganger in a way that merges contemporary debates with long-standing questions. By relying on traditional formulas, but altering (and, to a degree, subverting) them, this novel emphasizes both the malleability and durability of the doppelganger. The book also highlights the cultural anxiety related to technology vis-à-vis the narrative's reliance on the recording device that first alerts Tertuliano to the existence of his double and then, later, helps him learn his double's identity in order to track him down.

Reworking an Old Formula

Saramago's *The Double* echoes several earlier literary works that treat the motif of the double. The novel follows tradition insofar as it features two individuals who are not only look-a-likes, but who sound the same and share personality traits. Like much of the fiction that concerns literary doppelgangers, this novel also reflects the oft-repeated sentiment that "you are your own worst enemy"—especially because of the manner in which the story ends. The novel's last few pages describe the apparent death of Tertuliano's double, António Claro. Just as he starts to feel certain that António's death brings with it the promise of freedom, however, Tertuliano receives a mysterious phone call.

The man on the other end of the line claims to be his double; he speaks in a voice which sounds identical to Tertuliano's own and explains that he has been trying to reach him so the two can meet. Tertuliano agrees to meet him in a local park, but he brings a loaded gun along with him. Thus, the novel ends with Tertuliano's fate (not to mention the fate of the mysterious stranger) seemingly up in the air. The dark and also rather ambivalent manner in which this novel ends highlights the anxiety that has long-been associated with the figure of the double. Moreover, the novel points at a cause of this anxiety by suggesting that both fear of self and fear of annihilation are at its core. In this manner, Saramago's *The Double* is reminiscent of Poe's "William Wilson," which ends on a similarly dark note.

The formula that Saramago uses in his novel can also be seen quite clearly in Dostoevsky's 1846 novella *The Double*, which tells the story of a government clerk who goes insane as a result of his repeated encounters with his doppelganger. Much of the tension in that novella is a result of the internal psychological struggles that plague its main character, Yakov Petrovich Golyadkin. Like Dostoesky's novella, Saramago's *The Double* also recounts a man's descent into madness.

Clues to Tertuliano Máximo Afonso's fragile mental state can be found peppered throughout the narrative. It is worth noting that he appears depressed and aimless early in the novel, even before he spies his double in the film. He begins to behave quite strangely as soon as he spots his look-a-like and he soon becomes obsessed with his apparent double. To be sure, Tertuliano exhibits symptoms of obsessiveness, both in the way he scours videotapes to determine the identification of the man who appears to be his double and by tracking him down, all the while hiding the existence of his doppelganger from those close to him.

Indeed, as John Banville points out, "the lengths to which Tertuliano goes to conceal the existence of his double from those closest to him, principally his girlfriend and his mother, make one suspect he is suffering from something more serious than a 'temporary weakness of spirit.'" Moreover, the fact that "there is someone in the city who is not only his mirror image but, as it turns out, his exact double terrifies" him (Banville). The combined effect is that Tertuliano soon appears to be a man driven by obsession and governed by his feelings of fear and paranoia.

While there is some debate about how best to interpret Saramago's *The Double* (as well as disagreement about the book's literary merits), critics and reviewers do tend to agree that the novel clearly reworks an old formula. For instance, in his article "Twins in a Spin," which he published in *The Guardian*, Alberto Manguel notes that José Saramago is "obviously fond of rewriting old tales. Whether a different version of Christ's Passion (*The Gospel According to Jesus Christ*) or another account of the universal scourge (*Blindness*), Saramago has found in these primordial narratives fodder for his own fictional world. His new novel, *The Double*, continues this echoing tradition." Banville seems to agree that Saramago follows tradition in this novel. He describes Saramago's take on the theme of the double as "clever, alarming and blackly funny" (Banville). Although John Updike's view of the novel diverges to an extent from both Manguel's and Banville's, he nonetheless recognizes Saramago as following in a long literary tradition through his depiction of the doppelganger figure. He also views Saramago's use of the trope as part of a larger and thorough "investigation of human nature" that he undertakes in the novel (Updike).

The Role of Technology

In *The Double*, Saramago revises a formula that can be found in earlier literary works, and he thus borrows from traditional representations of the figure of the literary doppelganger. Nonetheless, his novel differs from these depictions because of the central role played by technology—in particular because of Saramago's reliance upon a VCR and numerous video recorded copies of movies, all of which not only serve as important plot devices but also have a symbolic function.

It should be noted that in *The Double* the protagonist first sees his doppelganger via the lens of technology, since he catches sight of his look-a-like by watching a video recording of a movie on his home VCR. Unlike early literary representations of doubles, which so often highlight the tension between nature and the supernatural, in *The Double*, because Tertuliano first observes his doppelganger via a video recording, the novel sets up a different type of tension, one related to technology.

After Tertuliano spies his double in the movie, he grows obsessed and decides to track down his look-a-like. Since his doppelganger has just a minor acting role in the film, Tertuliano is not able to immediately identify him. He methodically proceeds to watch all the films made by the same production company in order to decipher the identity of the actor with whom he shares a face. Through a complicated process of elimination (Tertuliano studies the cast lists in the credits of the films in which his double appears and those in which he does not), he finally establishes that the actor performs under the name Daniel Santa-Clara. In the course of this pursuit, Tertuliano learns that the actor going by the name Daniel Santa-Clara has played small roles in a number of films and it becomes clear to him, as well, that the two men share more than just a physical resemblance: Tertuliano and his double also have the same voice and mannerisms.

Again, Tertuliano gleans all of this information via his VCR. One effect of this is that, by replicating Tertuliano's image in the form of the actor (his double) who appears—albeit in bit parts—in countless video recordings, Saramago creates a *mise-en-abîme*. For both Tertuliano and the novel's readers, the video recordings replicate the visual experience of standing between two mirrors and seeing as a result an infinite reproduction of the same image (the face of Terutliano's double, who appears, and reappears, on screen).

Another consequence of Tertuliano learning about his double via these videocassettes is that the technology that clues him in to his doppelganger's existence functions symbolically, as well, since, by its very nature, a videocassette is a recorded copy (of a performance or live event). This symbol strikes at the heart of Tertuliano's fear and pushes him to seek his double to find out who the original is and who the copy is. It is worth mentioning that, in the case of videocassettes, there really is no original, since they all exist as copies—albeit imperfect ones (limited by the very technology that creates them). This, too, points to a source of Tertuliano's anxiety and the novel's larger questions: What if Tertuliano's identity if nothing more than mere iterations or performances? What if his life—his very existence—is no more than a role he is playing, one that his double could try on and discard as easily as he performs those bit-parts in all of those movies?

The root of Tertuliano's dread is that he worries that there is no "self" behind his, or his double's, iterations of identity. Elaine L. Graham speaks about this particular sort of fear as part of her discussion of the many anxieties that are symptomatic of our fragmented, postmodern condition, including the fear that there is no "'self' behind the expressions and performances of identity" (193). Indeed, according to Kenneth Gergen, a sign of contemporary times is that identity is now thought of as being fluid. This fluidity challenges traditional notions of self by suggesting that identity is malleable rather than fixed—the effect is, though this new definition of self may be seen as a positive change in the minds of some individuals, this shift may operate as a source of tension for others.

For Tertuliano, this changing concept of identity serves as a source of tension—indeed, he seems to fear that there may be no such thing as "self" after all. In this respect, Saramago's protagonist also reflects—at the same time as he shines a light on—the contemporary fear that there is, actually, nothing at essence of the "self." Tertuliano worries that, just as Bruce M. Hood, Norbert Elias, and others who investigate psychological and sociological definitions of the self argue, we are all just products of those around us and the different storylines we inhabit.

Spurred to action by these fears, Tertuliano Máximo Afonso grows determined to find his double and confront him. He obtains the actor's address from the production company and also learns his double's real name: António Claro. Armed with this new knowledge, Tertuliano stalks and tracks down his double and eventually arranges a meeting with him.

Saramago's Depiction of Doubling as an Irreconcilable Tension

While Tertuliano does, indeed, meet up with his doppelganger, António Claro, their encounter, rather than solving problems, brings new difficulties. For starters, a rivalry seems to exist from the onset between the two.

After introducing themselves to each other, the two men compare notes and quickly ascertain that they are, in fact, identical to one another. Not only are they identical physically, but their voices are the same, as well. The two even share the same birth date. António, it seems, is driven by the same fear that plagues Tertuliano, namely that "one of them, either the actor or the history teacher, was superfluous in the world" (Saramago 303).

The lingering concern for both men is to determine who the "original" is (and, conversely, who the copy must be). With this in mind, António asks Tertuliano the exact time of his birth. When Tertuliano reveals he was born at two o'clock in the afternoon, António retorts that was born earlier, and so he must therefore be the "original." The two then part with harsh words.

The tension between the two men grows, and it eventually not only consumes them, but affects their significant others, as well, since António ends up following Maria (Tertuliano's girlfriend, who is unaware of what is going on) and, in response, Tertuliano hatches a plan to sleep with António's wife, Helena. Their scheming brings about tragedy, since Maria and António end of dying in the same car accident. Tertuliano, shaken by what's occurred, but also wanting to put it behind him, returns to António's house and confesses the truth to Helena. He admits what's happened and explains how her husband has died as a result of the accident.

Although she is clearly upset, Helena invites Tertuliano to take the place of her husband. Just as he is easing into his new life, Tertuliano, receives a phone call which unsettles him. The mysterious caller claims to be his double and demands to see him. The novel then concludes on an open-ended note, with Tertuliano on the way to this meeting and his fate very much up in the air. By ending the novel in such an uncertain manner, Saramago leaves the tension that has so long plagued Tertuliano unresolved. Moreover, rather than offering concrete answers to the questions he raises in the novel about identity, he presents an ambivalent message about its nature.

At the same time as he raises timely and provocative questions about identity, Saramago also demonstrates the elasticity of the figure of the doppelganger. Although his use of the trope hearkens back to traditional representations of the archetypal figure, he departs from these earlier representations in the way he relies on technology—specifically the VCR and many VHS tapes which remain important to the plot—to interrogate the nature of identity. Moreover, the novel's reliance on these forms of technology as symbols works to highlight Tertuliano's fear—as well as the cultural anxiety connected to it—that identity is performative and nothing more.

3. The Ethics of Cloning in Kazuo Ishiguro's *Never Let Me Go*

Another novel that remains invested in exploring identity is *Never Let Me Go* (2005), written by Kazuo Ishiguro; however, unlike Saramago, the questions of identity are brought to the forefront in Ishiguro's novel due to treatment of the subject of human cloning. Ishiguro was born in Japan in 1954, but he moved with his family to England in 1960. Now one of the most renowned authors writing in English, Ishiguro was awarded the Man Booker Prize for his 1989 novel, *The Remains of the Day*. He has also written numerous screenplays and short stories, as well as other novels, including his work of speculative fiction, *Never Let Me Go*, which is a clone narrative about the ethics of cloning. Although many classify the novel within the genre of science fiction—and Ishiguro clearly borrows many traits from the genre in the fictional world he imagines—he eschews a futuristic setting; instead, the events of *Never Let Me Go* take place in Britain in a dystopian, alternate version of the 1990s.

Never Let Me Go follows protagonist Kathy H., a clone who now works as a "carer," offering comfort as well as medical assistance to other clones whose organs are being harvested as replacement parts. For much of the novel, Kathy looks back to the time she spent with her friends, Tommy and Ruth (who are also clones); many of these flashbacks are from the years they lived at Hailsham, a special boarding school, while other memories are of the time spent at place called the Cottages, a residential community where they later lived.

Some of Kathy's flashbacks pertain to her close friend Ruth's search for her double. Ruth, after hearing that a "possible" for her lives nearby, ventures out with a group of friends in an attempt to find this "possible," an older woman who is rumored to resemble Ruth and thus could be the woman from whom she was cloned. While at its core, *Never Let Me Go* is a novel that serves as a cautionary tale about the ethics of cloning and was written in response to the successful cloning of Dolly the sheep (who was cloned in 1996), by including a subplot about Ruth's search for her double, the book nevertheless reiterates the theme of "the search for self," which can so frequently be seen in storylines that feature the trend of doppelgangers.

Cloning, Controversy and Consequences

At its root, Ishiguro's *Never Let Me Go* is a clone narrative and thus a science fiction story concerned with human rights issues. According to Titus Levy, who addresses the book in his article "Human Rights Storytelling and Trauma Narrative in Kazuo Ishiguro's *Never Let Me Go*," throughout the novel, Ishiguro presents coded models of contemporary human rights issues in order to bring these issues into debate. Though Levy and other critics have noted how Ishiguro's novel works well as a broad discussion about human rights in a world full of continually emerging medical technologies, the book raises specific ethical questions about the practice of cloning. As Leona Toker and Daniel Chertoff highlight in their article "Reader Response and the Recycling of Topoi in Kazuo Ishiguro's *Never Let Me Go*," *Never Let Me Go* is a novel with "peculiarly contemporary ethical implications" (163).

The novel was, in fact, written in response to the cloning of Dolly, the infamous female domestic sheep, who, in 1996, was the first animal to be cloned from an adult somatic cell using the process of nuclear transfer. The fact that the situation its characters face gets imagined in response to this recent scientific breakthrough sets Ishiguro's novel apart from others with respect to its timeliness. Indeed, the novel's themes communicate much to us about our contemporary cultural anxieties. As science fiction author Cory Doctorow emphasizes in his article which appears in *Slate*,

> The science fiction stories that we remember—such as *Frankenstein*—are ones that resonate with the public imagination. Most science fiction is forgotten shortly after it's published, but a few of those tales live on for years, decades—even centuries in the case of *Frankenstein*. The fact that a story captures the public imagination doesn't mean that it will come true in the future, but it tells you something about the *present*. You learn something about the world when a vision of the future becomes a subject of controversy or delight.

In this manner, *Never Let Me Go* thus confronts the contemporary controversy of cloning, which caught the public's attention due to the successful cloning of Dolly, the sheep.

Yet, at the same time as he engages with contemporary debates, Ishiguro also looks ahead at the potential problems the practice might bring with it. Indeed, in *Never Let Me Go* Ishiguro imagines cloning taken just a few steps further since, in his fictional world, technology has advanced to the point that scientists can successfully clone human beings. Thus, a new class of humans exist: clones, whose sole purpose is to provide replacement parts for others. Kathy H., the book's protagonist, is one such clone. She has been raised in a special boarding school called Hailsham, where she has been conditioned to accept her lot. Margaret Atwood, who discusses Kathy's experiences, as well as the fate that awaits her and other clones, explains:

> Hailsham exists to raise cloned children who have been brought into the world for the sole purpose of providing organs to other, "normal" people. They don't have parents. They can't have children. Once they graduate, they will go through a period of being "carers" to others of their kind who are already being deprived of their organs; then they will undergo up to four "donations" themselves, until they "complete."

As this description highlights, Kathy H. and the other clones exist solely so their vital organs can serve as replacement parts for others. They lack autonomy and agency (even control over their own bodies) and have thus been systematically denied the basic human rights so many take for granted.

The science fiction lens and dystopian setting of Ishiguro's novel open up spaces to discuss these ethical concerns—and they rely upon the concept of doubling to do so. Toker and Chertoff, who nonetheless situate the novel in the genre of dystopian fiction, contend that Ishiguro reshapes the conventions of that genre by the way the book takes part in a sustained discussion of "modern concerns with cloning and organ transplant" (163). Indeed, there is a tinge of social protest to Ishiguro's novel, which also serves as a cautionary tale about biomedical technology taken too far. Thus, Ishiguro, as these remarks suggest, also plays with—at the same time as he relies upon—genre as part of his project of showing the ethical issues at stake.

To be sure, representations of human cloning provoke cultural anxieties about identity while also raising important ethical questions about what constitutes humanity. Yet, at the same time, these depictions also bring to the forefront questions about the treatment—as well as the legal and moral status—of beings such as clones. As Rachel Carroll, who discusses the novel in her article "Imitations of Life: Cloning, Heterosexuality and the Human in Kazuo Ishiguro's *Never Let Me Go*," notes, contemporary debates about the prospect of reproductive cloning often address how "copies" of human originals (such as clones) challenge notions of the human (59). This is especially the case in relation to issues of individuality, authenticity, and origin (Carroll 59).

As a clone narrative, *Never Let Me Go* raises questions about the nature of clones as beings by pondering, for instance, whether they are fully human—as well as by considering their legal and moral status. To be sure, at the same time as Ishiguro's novel poses these ontological and legal questions, *Never Let Me Go* also debates ethical concerns related to the treatment of clones. In recent years, discussion about the implications of cloning humans have included many ethical arguments against the practice, including frequently touted concerns about the status of cloned beings and moral objections to the way cloning could potentially transform procreation into a manufacturing process. Sophia M. Kolehmainen, who discusses the issue in "Human Cloning: Brave New Mistake," adds to this list the argument that cloning would lead to the "commodification of humans."

Kazuo Ishiguro's novel—albeit at times only implicitly—reflects these same concerns since the scenario he imagines in his fictional world show these dangers come to life. As Amit Marcus emphasizes in the article "Telling the Difference: Clones, Doubles and what's in Between," *Never Let Me Go* addresses how "spectacular scientific achievements of the modern era are not necessarily followed by similar progress in ethics" (367). Moreover, the novel also showcases "potential abuses of biotechnology by narcissistic individuals, totalitarian regimes, and dehumanizing societies" (Marcus 367).

While some critics read the novel as a mere metaphor about the dangers of scientific breakthroughs run amuck, others, such as Gabriele Griffin, who addresses the novel in "Science and the Cultural Imaginary: The Case of Kazuo Ishiguro's *Never Let Me Go*," resist relegating the novel to "the realm of metaphor," insisting, instead, that *Never Let Me God* is a warning against "the dehumanized normalization" of the ethical atrocities that science can cause (652). Tiffany Tsao, who discusses the book in her article "The Tyranny of Purpose: Religion and Biotechnology in Ishiguro's *Never Let Me Go*," agrees. She emphasizes that the society that Ishiguro constructs in the novel is "obviously the fictional counterpart of our society with its recent breakthroughs in cloning and stem-cell technology" (Tsao 220).

Never Let Me Go, indeed, works well as a cautionary tale about the dangers of human cloning, especially by using its characters and their predicaments to illustrate how the practice de-values life and is dehumanizing. While the novel paints a rather disheartening picture of the practice of human cloning, protagonist Kathy H., curiously, does not reflect on the practice with the amount of horror we might expect. Rather, she speaks of her time at Hailsham fondly, and she even goes as far as to "resist smugness rather than protesting" her situation, a point that John Mullan argues (105). Indeed, Kathy H. "thinks herself, knows herself, privileged" (Mullan 105).

Although Kathy reflects a degree of awareness about her role in the dystopian society that Ishiguro creates, she comes across as, by and large, "undisturbed by what she narrates," as Martin Puchner notes in "When We Were Clones" (36). Puchner argues that her apparent "lack of outrage more than anything else makes one wonder whether she is not somehow deficient, perhaps in a way one might expect from a manufactured creature" (36). Puchner's comments highlight the fact that the novel also sets Kathy H. and other clones apart from other humans by the manner in which they reflect upon their situation.

This same quality, however, also works as part of the novel's criticism of the practice of human cloning—and a warning of its consequences. Beyond the fact that the process of creating human clones in order to harvest their organs is ethically dubious, there is the attendant issue about the rights of beings whose status—legal, moral, and ontological—is uncertain. The clones that populate Ishiguro's novel are undoubtedly human-like, but are they human?

Even in the case of Kathy H., whose thoughts readers have access to (since she is the book's narrator), there remains ambiguity about this issue. As Puchner describes it, in "Kathy H., Ishiguro has created a voice that hovers, uncannily, on the edge of the human" (36). Curiously, Kathy can create art, read Shakespeare, and provide care to others—in fact, she prides herself on being a good "carer," admitting she has "a great record" looking after other clones who are undergoing multiple surgeries (so that their organs can be transplanted to others)—yet, it seems, she has also largely resigned herself to her fate as she unquestioningly accepts that she will soon "finish" her career, which euphemistically means she herself will become an organ donor soon (Ishiguro 3–4). Indeed, neither Kathy H. nor her fellow clones, who apparently have at least a chance to escape, were they to try, openly question the system. Instead, they submit to the process of "donation," just as they have been conditioned to do.

Yet, by pushing readers to question "the status of the clone," Ishiguro, by extension, also forces us to examine the notion of the human (Puchner 37). Part of the argument against cloning resides in the fear that the practice will strip humans of their individuality—and hence their identity. In 2002 (just a few years after the successful cloning of Dolly (the sheep)— and a few years prior to the publication of Ishiguro's novel), the President's Council on Bioethics included the following statement in response to questions posed about cloning to produce human children:

> The character of sexual procreation shapes the lives of children as well as parents. By giving rise to genetically new individuals, sexual reproduction imbues all human beings with a sense of individual identity and of occupying a place in this world that has never belonged to another. Our novel genetic identity symbolizes and foreshadows the unique, never-to-be-repeated character of each human life. At the same time, our emergence from the union of two individuals, themselves conceived and generated as we were, locates us immediately in a network of relation and natural affection.

As this statement makes clear, part of being human stems from having a unique genetic identity; according to this definition, clones, by their very nature, trouble these boundaries. To be sure, even though *Never Let Me Go* is a book about the ethics of cloning, the book also brings up debates about what it means to be human. Indeed, as Maria Aline Seabra Ferreira argues in in *I am the Other: Literary Negotiations of Human Cloning*, cloned humans "challenge commonly held perceptions about our own bodies and our relations to other bodies" (2). In this way, clones, in fact, call into question what it means to be human.

The Search for Self

What constitutes human individuality? What makes one human being unique from all others? These age-old questions are still being explored today. Just as Corey L. Guenther and Mark D. Alick outline in "Psychology and the Self," the "self" is undoubtedly one of the most debated notions in social and personality psychology—and there is even disagreement as to whether a "self" truly exists. Yet, whatever "stance one adopts regarding the self's ontological status, there is little doubt that the many phenomena of which the self is a predicate—self-knowledge, self-awareness, self-esteem, self-enhancement, self-regulation, self-deception, self-presentation—to name just a few" (Guenther and Alick).

While *Never Let Me Go* clearly functions as a cautionary tale about the ethics of cloning, the novel also includes the theme of "the search for self." These concerns, which are raised side-by-side in the novel, are actually connected, not least of all because they both relate to the concept of doubling. This connection comes to light by looking at two sets of memories from Kathy's childhood.

In the first memory, Kathy H. relates how, at Hailsham, they have been told since they were children—even before they could process such information—that they exist solely to fulfill their role as donors. At one point, she describes Miss Lucy (who works at the school) telling the Hailsham students: "Your lives are set out for you. You'll become adults, then before you're old, before you're even middle-aged, you'll start to donate your vital organs. That's what each of you was created to do" (Ishiguro 80). In another passage, Kathy confides how, armed with the knowledge that they were made as copies of others, the children at Hailsham fantasized about finding their "possibles." As Mullan explains it, at Hailsham, students would "talk with each other about their 'possibles theory,' the idea that for each of them there must be a person from which he or she had been copied" (104). Kathy spells out the different theories that were raised: "some students thought you should be looking for a person twenty to thirty years older than yourself—the sort of age a normal parent would be. But others claimed this was sentimental" (Ishiguro 137).Years later, Kathy's friend Ruth hears a rumor that there is a "possible" for her living close by and, spurred on by these childhood fantasies, seeks out her double.

The sequence of events take place as follows: neighbors (fellow clones) in the Cottages, the residential community where Ruth, Kathy, and Tommy live, spot someone in nearby Norfolk who they think looks like Ruth. They tell Ruth what they have seen, thinking this woman might be the "original" from whom Ruth was copied. Ruth is curious and excited after hearing this rumor, so she travels to town with her friends to get a glimpse of this "possible." When they catch sight of the woman, however, Ruth and they others all agree that any resemblance they share is merely superficial.

Disappointed by this realization, and also agitated—but neither able to comprehend nor process the source of her anger—at the sight of this woman living a "normal" life, Ruth lashes out: "We're modelled from *trash*. Junkies, prostitutes, winos, tramps. Convicts, maybe, just so long as they aren't psychos. That's what we come from. We all know it, so why don't we say it?" (Ishiguro 166). Ruth also expresses incredulity that they, even for a moment, thought that this woman could have been a "clone model," lamenting to her friends, "If you want to look for possibles, if you want to do it properly, then you look in the gutter. You look in rubbish bins.

Look down the toilet, that's where you'll find where we all came from" (Ishiguro 166).

As her emotional reaction makes clear, far from finding the answers she wants, Ruth's search for self leads her down a dark path. Indeed, just as she is confronted by the stark reality of their shared situation, she grows upset, and, in turn, antagonizes her friends with the implications of her frustrated and unsuccessful quest. In many ways, this futile journey to Norfolk works symbolically to suggest not only Ruth's failure, but the failure of any of the clones to establish an identity.

Questions of Identity: A New Take on an Old Debate

Whether through Ruth's search for self—which Kathy narrates—or through his reliance on the concept of cloning, Kazuo Ishiguro uses the trope of the doppelganger to engage with enduring existential debates while also addressing current controversies about emerging medical technologies. Indeed, what the search for the self and cloning have in common is both relate to the concept of doubling—and, as passages from the novel make clear, Ishiguro, relies on these same concerns to discuss a number of related questions. His characters, for instance, both implicitly and explicitly debate complex questions, such as: What constitutes humanity? Is there such thing as a soul, and how do you know if you have one?

At the root of these debates lie questions about what it means to be human. To be sure, as Margaret Atwood points out, in *Never Let Me Go*, Ishiguro tackles a "difficult subject: ourselves, seen through a glass darkly." This novel thus brings to bear concerns about human nature and existence by calling into question the traits humans most value—our autonomy, individualism, and self-expression—notions which are being challenged and redefined in the contemporary era. The result is that *Never Let Me Go* works as both a novel about the ethics of cloning and as a cultural product which highlights 21st century cultural anxieties about the changing concept of the self.

4. Through a Machine Darkly: Blake Crouch's *Dark Matter*

While *Never Let Me Go* is a narrative which relies on fictional representations of human cloning to debate the changing nature of identity in our postmodern world, Blake Crouch's 2016 science fiction novel *Dark Matter* uses another popular science fiction trope, the existence of parallel universes, to call attention to how identity is being redefined in contemporary times. Alongside his use of this trope, Crouch also relies on the literary motif of the double to reflect 21st century cultural anxieties and to address how identity is being challenged and contested in the contemporary era.

Born in 1978 in North Carolina, Crouch currently works as a novelist and screenwriter. While he is perhaps best known for his *Wayward Pines* trilogy on which the recent television series was based, Crouch has also penned a number of other works including *Dark Matter*, where he imagines a multiverse populated by near infinite versions of the same individual. That individual is the novel's protagonist and narrator, community college professor Jason Dessen, who learns about the existence of parallel universes after a series of strange events unfold.

The complicated chain of events begin when he is rendered unconscious and abducted, only to then be taken against his will to an alternate universe. He wakes up tied to a gurney surrounded by people who claim to know him. Jason Dessen, however, does not recognize these people, nor does he understand why he has been brought to the unfamiliar site. It turns out that he has been transported by a futuristic piece of technology, and that the world he lands in is one where he made a different set of choices earlier in his life by focusing on his career, rather than his family.

While a hypothesis gets floated around that Jason Dessen is suffering from some sort of amnesia, he soon discovers the truth: he has, in fact, unwittingly switched places (so to speak) with a double of himself. This alternate Jason Dessen, who is referred to in the novel as Jason 2, is a brilliant, internationally celebrated quantum physicist who has found a way to monetize his scientific innovations. Although he is recognized for his intelligence and is financially well-off in this timeline, prime Jason Dessen quickly realizes how badly he misses his wife Daniela and son Charlie, so he tries to find a way home. In the course of trying to return to his family, he learns that it was, in fact, his doppelganger who was responsible for separating him from his family and, thus, he must face off against him. Moreover, he must also confront many other versions of himself to fight his way home.

Technology and Identity

The title of Blake Crouch's science fiction novel alludes to the dark power of technology and it also refers to the machine which transports Jason Dessen between dimensions by using dark energy (or dark matter) as its fuel source. While this machine is quite powerful—it has to be to allow travel between dimensions of space—it also serves as a source of anxiety for Jason Dessen since it has the potential to separate him from everything he knows and loves. The novel's title, however, also alludes to the shadow side of Jason Dessen, a side which he must confront in order to return home. Like dark matter, which emits no light and cannot be directly observed (but which scientists believe makes up much of the mass of the universe), *Dark Matter*'s protagonist has many darker impulses which are not superficially discernible. Rather than portraying these as internal psychological conflicts, Crouch (using the plot device of parallel universes) brings these confrontations to life by having the prime Jason Dessen literally face off against other versions of himself.

Prime Jason Dessen has to negotiate multiple timelines on his journey home; every time he enters and departs another dimension, a new version of himself is created, who then makes slightly different decisions—and this occurs in a seemingly endless cycle. Hence, each possible version of Jason who enters (and later leaves) each reality becomes another person made flesh—and a number of these Jasons make their way back to prime Jason's timeline (what each one sees as his reality). Thus, in the novel, Jason Dessen must ponder the nature of reality while also confronting different versions of himself—and, he must also grapple with the many questions related to identity that these various encounters inevitably bring up.

To be sure, as the novel's title as well as its plot suggest, *Dark Matter* is a narrative about identity and the choices we make. Nonetheless, the novel is also fraught with concerns about both the perils and promises that new forms of technology bring. Ultimately, Crouch merges these concerns, which helps him to call attention to contemporary society's conflicted feelings about the impact technology has on human lives. His novel thus reveals our cultural ambivalence, which is symptomatic of the identity crisis taking place in our era.

Many Copies, Multiple Realities

In *Dark Matter*, Crouch imagines a scenario in which a quantum physicist creates a machine which allows him to travel between dimensions. Thus, in the novel, the "quantum many-worlds theory has become a fully realized technology for interdimensional transfer" (Daniels 34). This technology, which basically opens doors to multiple, parallel universes, operates both a plot device and as a means to justify the existence of so many doubles. Moreover, the machine works as a way to forward the novel's action since it is because of the machine that prime Jason Dessen gets transported to a parallel universe in the first place—and it is also the mechanism by which he attempts to return home. Moreover, the machine is responsible, in part, for making manifest his multiplicity (since every time he enters into and departs from a dimension, another version of himself gets created), a plot detail which highlights the relationship between technology and multiplicity.

In writing this novel, Crouch echoes a formula that has long been a hallmark of science fiction. Not only is the doppelganger a "frequent theme of science fiction," but, as David Deutsch explains in *The Beginning of Infinity: Explanations That Transform The World*, there also exists a formula where, rather than copying from an original to create a doppelganger, a double "exists from the outset in a parallel universe" and the two can "communicate or even travel to meet" one another." This pattern is one which Crouch relies upon in *Dark Matter*. Indeed, just as Andrew Liptak asserts, "multiple realities is a long-standing trope within science fiction, and Crouch isn't the first to play with the idea." Yet, in *Dark Matter*, Crouch's "particular vision of the multiverse," as Alison Flood points out, is "posited on the Schrodinger's cat experiment—'you figured out a way to turn a human being into a living and dead cat,' Jason is told at one point. Here, the choices we make splinter off into new worlds all the time."

Writing for *The New York Times*, Andrew O'Hehir also comments on how Crouch relies upon the "multiple realities" convention of the science fiction genre, noting that, thanks to a "light dusting of pop physics—specifically, the 'many worlds' version of multiverse theory, in which virtually every choice made by every sentient being engenders a new universe," Crouch uses a familiar formula to explore the choices we make. In fact, Crouch himself readily acknowledges that, in writing *Dark Matter*, he wanted to explore the degree to which we are our choices. Crouch explains this in an interview he gave about the book:

> What interested me most about this dynamic was how a relationship between two people might change based upon different choices they'd made in their past. In other words, would my relationship with my partner be markedly different if I were a mechanic instead of a writer? Are we still the same people on a far deeper level? Would we share the same connection, even if our respective histories were completely different? [Daniels 34].

As these remarks by novelist Blake Crouch highlight, *Dark Matter* remains, at its core, a novel about how the decisions we make both shape and reveal facets of ourselves. Crouch uses the plot device of parallel universes—and the existence of the countless doppelgangers that the multiverse theory engenders—to bring questions such as these to the forefront.

After seeing several of the other paths he could have gone down, Jason Dessen begins to understand how the life he has been living was the outcome of his priorities and the choices he made. In his timeline, he sacrificed many of his professional aspirations to settle down and raise a family. Although he did not entirely give up his career—he has a comfortable job teaching at a community college in the Chicago area—he did set aside his more lofty scientific pursuits in order to focus on family. In contrast, Jason 2 gave up his chance to have a family in order to—ruthlessly and relentlessly, it turns out—commit to scientific pursuits. While Jason 2 achieved fame and financial success for his efforts, his choices nonetheless left him lonely.

Prime Jason Dessen (again, thanks to the technology that allows him to explore other timelines) also catches sight of numerous other iterations of himself, prompting him to come to this conclusion: "If I represent the pinnacle of family success for all the Jason Dessens, Jason 2 represents the professional and creative apex" (Crouch 227). In the novel, the multiverse formula (along with the existence of his many doppelgangers) pushes protagonist Jason Dessen to reach this conclusion. As O'Hehir explains it, Crouch is "effectively repurposing and joining two well-worn channels of fictional speculation," one being "the idea of another universe as an inverted or ironic reflection of ours, as in the movie *Sliding Doors* or the *Star Trek* episode featuring an evil, bearded Spock or the Philip K. Dick classic *The Man in the High Castle*." To be sure, notions of personal choice and identity are at the heart of Blake Crouch's novel—and these are the same questions that his protagonist wrestles with. Since the "Jasons are almost identical," while prime Jason "struggles to find his way home," he must also come to "terms with everything about his life that made it *his*, flaws and all. What makes him *him*" (Liptak).

Jason Dessen himself, in fact, explicitly poses this question, when he asks, "If you strip away all the trappings of personality and lifestyle, what are the core components that make me *me*?" (Crouch 218). This question propels him in his search for self, a quest frequently represented by the motif of the literary doppelganger. Just as O'Herir argues, within the book, there is clearly the echo of "the literary conceit, going back at least as far as Poe and Dostoevsky and Henry James, that throughout our lives we remain haunted by what we might have been, by the ghosts of people we never became."

When he first appears in the novel, prime Jason Dessen seems plagued by these very concerns. For a moment, spurred to jealousy at the news that a colleague has been awarded a prestigious prize, he wonders what he might have achieved under different circumstances. He does not have to wait long for an answer to that question, though, since later that same night he gets kidnapped, drugged, and transported to an alternate dimension, one where he is able to see all of his scientific visions brought to life. Prime Jason Dessen's career has been greatly eclipsed by Jason 2's creative and professional successes, so this world has much to offer him. Nonetheless, when faced with the possibility of losing his wife and his son Charlie, prime Jason realizes that there is too high of a cost to this existence.

At one point, he goes as far as to wonder, "Will I keep fighting to be the man I think I am? Or will I disown him and everything he loves, and step into the person this world would like for me to be?" (Crouch 23). While the lifestyle Jason 2 leads holds some allure, ultimately prime Jason Dessen decides that he wants nothing more than to return home. Yet, finding his way home means again using the technology his doppelganger created— and it also means having to confront many versions of himself.

Some of these doubles have clearly fared far worse than prime Jason Dessen (indeed, other of his doppelgangers live in worlds that have been decimated by war or environmental disasters), so he also must come to terms with the many startling things he sees, including the desperate lengths some of his doubles will go to in order to get what they want. To be sure, he himself becomes more desperate as the novel progresses, and he must also make increasingly difficult choices to stay alive to have the chance to return home. Yet, amidst the chaos and confusion that confronting so many doubles across different timelines inevitably creates, he realizes that he and his doppelgangers share much in common: "We all want the same thing—to get our life back" (Crouch 262).

Representations of Doubles: From Tradition to Technology

To be sure, to forward the action of the narrative as well as to engage with concerns related to identity, the plot of *Dark Matter* relies heavily on the literary motif of the doppelganger. To an extent, Crouch relies upon traditional representations in his portrayal, especially in the way he uses Jason Dessen's many doubles to dramatize prime Jason's internal psychological struggles and bring to life the consequences of the choices he makes. Referring to how the motif frequently gets deployed in literature, Morteza Jafari argues in the article "Freud's Uncanny" that the figure of the "double refers to a representation of the ego that can assume various forms: shadow, reflection, portrait, and twin" (43). This same range of representation is clearly at work in the novel, *Dark Matter*, since Crouch dramatizes how prime Jason Dessen gets confronted by these various forms of the double as he traverses multiple realities. Moreover, in the novel, he also dramatizes the contradictory nature of the self, thus highlighting the potential that normally lies dormant in an individual.

In this sense, the novel reflects traditional ways the figure appears in literature (going back to the many literary accounts that have appeared over the centuries). *Dark Matter*, however, also echoes the sentiment that "you are your own worst enemy," since prime Jason Dessen can blame one of his doppelgangers (Jason 2, who created the machine) for causing his initial predicament. He also has reason to fear so many of his other doppelgangers since they clearly pose threats (not just to him, but also to his family's safety) and stand in his way of reuniting with his family. In this manner, Crouch's representation of the double in *Dark Matter* calls attention to the anxieties that have often been associated with the figure of the double: the fear of self and the fear of annihilation.

Beyond echoing traditional literary representations of the trope, ones that have long been in existence, Crouch also relies on a subset of the figure specific to the genre of science fiction. He creates an imaginative variation of the "allohistorical doppelgänger," a figure which can be found as far back as in the mid–20th century (in fact, the "allohistorical doppelgänger" first appeared in 1939, when L. Sprague De Camp published his dystopian novel, *Lest Darkness Fall*). According to Dennis Kogel and Irene Schäfer, who discuss the figure in "The Doppelgänger Motif in Science Fiction Film," the allohistorical doppelganger makes an appearance in narratives "featuring time travel and parallel universes" (138).

Their definition derives, in part, from Frank Dietz, who identifies different ways the figure has been brought to life in fiction. As part of his discussion of the trope, Dietz addresses the particular subset of the figure of the allohistorical doppelganger, a term which refers to the figure when it appears in narratives about parallel worlds or alternate histories (209–210). According to Dietz, a hallmark of this type of fiction is that it presents for readers alternative realities, whether through depictions of time travel, parallel universes, or alternative histories.

In each case, the effect is the same: "the allohistorical novel de-centers both characters and the levels of reality in a vision of a universe of infinite possibilities" (Dietz 216). As Dietz notes, reading allohistory also enables us to face "our utopian selves and measure something of what might have been" (Dietz 214). Indeed, as Dietz underscores, "allohistorical fiction deals with the question of what might have been" (214). Yet, he is quick to clarify that "the appeal of allohistorical fiction is that it is not so much concerned with alternative histories, but with our own society" (Dietz 214).

A hallmark of allohistorical fiction is that when doppelgangers appear, there is an emphasis "on nurture over nature," since these narratives often call attention to the large role environment plays in shaping identity (Kogel and Schäfer 138). Nonetheless, as Kogel and Schäfer are quick to point out, allohistorical doppelgangers that appear via the many-worlds interpretation acknowledge "an autonomous place for the doppelgänger," thus suggesting that these forms of doubles—rather than existing as mere copies—reflect a range of possibilities in terms of self-expression (Kogel and Schäfer 138).

This range can clearly be seen in *Dark Matter* due to the existence of prime Jason Dessen and his many counterparts, who, together, reflect a range of possible paths. As different versions of the same man, the diverse incarnations of Jason Dessen represented in this narrative call attention to the role experiences and environment play in shaping identity. It is worth noting that a similar dynamic can also be seen in many other contemporary science fiction texts (indeed, the novel *Version Control* and the television series *Fringe*, both of which are discussed in this book, also feature allohistorical doppelgangers and thus bring these concerns to bear, as well).

Although Blake Crouch relies on traditional representations of the doppelganger figure to inform his treatment of Jason Dessen and his many doubles, his novel also introduces concerns related to technology and highlights the cultural ambivalence we feel about its impact on our lives. Indeed, his novel showcases dilemmas that scholars and cultural historians like Donna Haraway, Bruno Latour, and Timothy Taylor reference in their discussions about the connection between human beings and our technology. In particular, Crouch's novel highlights the degree to which human beings have been co-evolving—and, indeed, continue to co-evolve—with our technology.

Certainly, in *Dark Matter*, technology, for better or worse, makes Jason Dessen who he is (on both a professional and personal level). Moreover, in the novel, technology is key to his self-awareness since it allows the protagonist to go on an incredible voyage of self-discovery by bringing to life for him the consequences of his actions. In much the same manner, however, Crouch depicts technology as dangerous and difficult to navigate. Indeed, for Jason Dessen, technology brings with it threats and peril, which function in the novel as plot devices and to propel the action, but which also highlight cultural anxieties about technology and how it impacts us as individuals in the 21st century.

5. Technology and the Self in Dexter Palmer's *Version Control*

"If you change history, does that change you in turn?"—James Gleick, *Time Travel: A History*

This question posed by James Gleick is at the heart of Dexter Palmer's science fiction novel, *Version Control*. Indeed, as another recent science fiction novel concerned with the impact technology has on our lives, *Version Control* relies on the multiple universes theory and the existence of doubles that trope engenders—and thus, like Blake Crouch's *Dark Matter*, the novel also includes treatment of allohistorical doppelgangers. To be sure, like Crouch, Palmer relies on these themes to explore how the choices we make shape us. While in *Dark Matter*, where Jason Dessen, the novel's protagonist, travels through a large number of parallel universes and therefore must come face-to-face the many different versions of himself, in *Version Control*, characters are only loosely aware of the existence of their doppelgangers. The book's audience, however, is privy to three possible timelines, so readers of the novel therefore bear witness to how one tragic and pivotal event, which plays out three different ways in the novel, affects the book's main characters. In this manner, the novel highlights the degree to which choice and circumstance both reveal and shape facets of the self. To be sure, the novel also poses questions not only about our ability to shape history, but about history's role in shaping us as individuals.

American author Dexter Clarence Palmer lives in Princeton, New Jersey. An academic (Palmer earned a Ph.D. from Princeton University), he published his first novel, *The Dream of Perpetual Motion*, in 2010. In 2016, Palmer published his second novel, *Version Control*, a work of science fiction about the invention of a "causality violation device" (basically a time machine), which begins to alter the fabric of reality. Because of the existence of this technology, readers glimpse three possible realities and how the different situations in each affect the personalities and destinies of the novel's protagonists. As these plot details suggest, the novel uses the existence of parallel universes to engage with questions of identity and to explore different "possible lives" (Palmer 155). This novel also rather self-consciously reveals anxieties related to emerging technologies—what the novel frequently refers to as the tension surrounding "technological change" (Palmer 156). Though these concerns have long-existed, they not only still remain pervasive, but have taken on different forms in the 21st century.

The Depiction of Parallel Universes

In *Version Control*, Dexter Palmer relies on a familiar trope, that of the multiverse. Indeed, his imagined parallel universes call to mind other fictional depictions, most notably perhaps the film *Sliding Doors* (1998), directed by Peter Howitt. The storyline of *Sliding Doors*, in fact, shares much in common with *Version Control*. Starring Gwyneth Paltrow, its plot centers on a twenty-something woman whose career and relationship both hinge, unbeknownst to her, on whether or not she makes the train she is trying to catch. Due to the narrative's reliance on the trope of parallel universes, the film's audience is thus presented with two possible outcomes. As David Deutsch describes it, at its core, *Sliding Doors* is a movie which "interleaves two variants of a love story, following the fortunes of two instances of the same couple in two universes, which initially differ in one small detail."

There is a key difference, however, between *Version Control* and *Sliding Doors*. In Palmer's novel, the very technology that Philip Wright and his team create remains responsible for the existence of the fractured timelines (whereas in *Sliding Doors*, no scientific justification is given for the two timelines presented). This difference proves significant because it operates as a way for Palmer to bring debates about technology into debate while also positioning Philip Wright, his team, and even his wife Rebecca as agents of this technological change.

Thus, in addition to troubling traditional notions of the self and identity, *Version Control* also proves to be about the tensions that the development of new technologies bring about. The "causality violation device" that Philip Wright develops is at the heart of the novel. He pours his time and effort into creating and testing out this new technology, even at the expense of his personal life. Wright, in fact, behaves quite recklessly by disregarding the potential personal costs and consequences of this new technology. Moreover, he introduces his machine to the world without fully understanding its capabilities. To be sure, Philip Wright can neither control nor even fully comprehend the device which he has made. This situation, in particular, reveals the novel as a cautionary tale about the perils of (so-called) progress. It also highlight the degree to which scientific pursuits have the potential to run amok.

In the case of the various scenarios presented in *Version Control*, it becomes clear that Philip Wright himself is largely to blame for the havoc his device creates in each. Since he invented the device and continues to test and tweak the technology without understanding its capabilities, the changes the device makes across the fabric of time can be traced back to Wright and his team. Of interest, it is Rebecca Wright, rather than her husband, who finally begins to understand what her husband's invention can do. Finally realizing that the many changes that have been taking place—alterations to the timeline that she can only scarcely perceive, let alone understand—she decides to use her husband's invention to change history, once and for all. Rebecca thus deliberately enters the machine at the conclusion of Part II, believing—correctly it turns out—that she, thanks to her husband's device, has the power to change events. She chooses to go back in time and save her husband and son, an action which also means sacrificing herself. Rebecca's actions thus represent the dilemma of being subject to technology as being resolved by re-taking control of the same tools that have the power to also shape us. Indeed, in *Version Control*, the power of technology comes across as multifaceted, and Palmer thus uses his novel to represent our wider cultural ambivalence about its use. While Palmer eventually shows this tension as being reconciled, it comes at a high cost since Rebecca must give her own life to save her family and put things right.

Multiple Timelines and Changed Selves

As these details suggest, *Version Control* is a novel concerned with both technology and the choices we make. In the novel, different possibilities are presented as diverse potential paths for the book's main characters—and each possibility gets fleshed out in a distinct narrative strand.

The book is, in fact, divided into three sections—Part I, Part II, and a short Coda—with each presenting a different possible timeline. Each timeline pivots on a climactic car crash, which is the result of a malfunction with an automatic automobile (in Palmer's fictional world, self-driving cars are a reality—and a part of everyday life). The car accident seems to be unavoidable as it occurs in all three of the timelines.

Also, in each of the timelines, Sean Wright, the young son of Philip and Rebecca, has been disciplined at school, therefore prompting his school to call his home so that he can be picked up. In Part I and Part II, the scenario plays out in such a way that Rebecca is too inebriated to leave the house, while Philip is too busy at work to fetch the boy. Thus, the question is left open about who is behind the wheel and who survives the car crash which inevitably takes place. The novel circles back to this pivotal accident time and time again, with crucial details about who is involved and who survives being subject to revision.

Rebecca Wright is the focus of both Part I and Part II of the novel, with the narrative showing her living out two possible timelines. In Part I, she is depicted as being drunk and behind the wheel when she comes upon a traffic nightmare, which leads to a multivehicle pile-up. Her son Sean dies in the resulting car crash. The narrative thus centers on Rebecca and Philip's relationship woes in the years following this tragic accident—as they try to come to terms with their son's death. While Rebecca and her husband both survive in this timeline, they come across as just barely getting by. Both feel guilty for the roles they played in the accident, and they remain haunted by Sean's death, a tragedy which tests their marriage.

Philip blames his wife for her role in their son's death (since she was drinking when she got into the vehicle), but he also feels guilty that he was too busy at work to fetch the boy himself. Consequently, Philip seeks an escape by burying himself in his work. He retreats to his scientific pursuits and spends much time in his lab where he and his team are working hard—seemingly without result—on a "causality violation device." He has begun an extramarital affair with Alicia, a female colleague, which further drives a wedge between him and his wife. As a form of avoidance, Rebecca turns to alcohol and, like Philip, she also tries to keep busy with her job (she works for an on-line dating site). For her part, Rebecca is quite literally haunted by Sean's death. She wonders if events could have turned out differently—and the grief surrounding this loss pushes to the point that she sometimes feels she can sense his presence, even though, rationally, she knows he has died. In fact, a number of the novel's passages detail how Rebecca will, at times, catch sight of him out of the corner of her eye. She also admits that when she arrives home from being out, she expects to find him there. The loss of her son leaves her bereft and seeking answers. Indeed, he tells her husband at one point that she would give everything to "get things to turn out another way" (Palmer 232).

Part II of the novel plays out in a different manner. While the Wrights still receive a phone call from their son's school, it is Philip this time who picks up the boy since Rebecca has been drinking and does not want to get behind the wheel of the car. The traffic accident still takes place, but its outcome changes: Sean survives the crash while his father Philip perishes. Within this version of events, Rebecca channels her grief for her husband by focusing on other parts of her life. She tries hard to be a good mother to Sean while also more aggressively pursuing a career (in both realities, she works for an on-line dating service, but she has a more integral role in the company in the second timeline presented). Also, in this timeline, she and Alicia, her husband's colleague, become running partners and eventually grow to be close friends. Although Rebecca seems happier in this timeline, she nonetheless laments her husband's passing. She also grows increasing curious about the project he had been working on prior to his tragic death.

Beyond addressing the ways this climactic car crash impact the Wright family, the narrative also takes care to paint differences between the societies represented in each timeline of these timelines. Indeed, the different timeline features technologies unique to each, the politicians in power differ in each (Rebecca perceives this on some level, prompting her to speculate that the man in the role of President "seems like the wrong person"), and the overall milieu of each reality comes across as distinct, as well (Palmer 3). These changes are noticeable to certain characters in the book, who register these differences but are unable to explain. For instance, Rebecca will often "notice strange things" and feel overcome by a feeling that "people and places are not exactly what she remembers or expects them to be" (Heller).

This belief, that somehow things aren't quite right, affects several of the characters, but it is Rebecca who gets pushed to action by her feelings. Part II culminates with Rebecca making a momentous decision. She, prompted by a newfound conviction that her (late) husband's invention is at the root of the sense that the world is off kilter, decides to use this machine to try to fix history. With Alicia's help, she manages to gain access to the lab and, while Alicia distracts the guards, she enters the machine.

The consequences of this decision only become clear in the novel's Coda, where it is revealed that Rebecca successfully traveled back in time and altered events. She was therefore able to prevent the deaths of her husbands of son, but had to sacrifice herself in order to do so. While for a while, her sacrifice goes unnoticed by the others, when a corpse resembling the Rebecca he knew mysteriously appears, Philip Wright is able to piece together that she must have entered into the machine—and, in effect, created a doppelganger of herself—in order to revise history. Finally confronted with this realization, Phil Wright understands the grave potential his machine carries and decides to de-commission the device. Thus ends the novel.

Revising History and the Role of Technology

Traditionally, the exploration of doppelgangers in science fiction gives rise to basic "nature versus nurture" debates. When deployed in this manner, the figure raises questions about the roles environment and experiences play in shaping the self. The figure thus makes us question whether we are ourselves because of how we have been defined by our surroundings and experiences, or if there is something innate within ourselves that makes us what we are.

In *Version Control*, Palmer offers treatment of the theme of the self which suggests that we are, by and large, products of our circumstances. Indeed, at one point, the novel clearly spells out the degree we are shaped by our history by espousing the belief, which also gets presented in the novel as a core dilemma, "if you traveled back in time, you wouldn't get to be you anymore" (Palmer 212). Rather than minimizing its role in identity formation, according to Palmer's narrative, "history makes you who you are" (Palmer 212). This theory gets fleshed out through the changed versions of Rebecca Wright that get depicted in the book's differing narrative strands. Indeed, the Rebecca who takes center stage in Part I comes across as an almost entirely different person than the Rebecca who emerges in Part II.

While, through and through, Palmer's novel remains concerned with identity, on a fundamental level, *Version Control* is also about the terrifying potential of technology. Palmer depicts the machine Philip Wright and his team create as both dangerous and difficult to navigate. The machine is portrayed as threatening, as well, because even the scientists who create it do not really comprehend it. This detail only further underscores the tension and uncertainty that new technologies often introduce.

To be sure, in Palmer's fictional world, technology brings with it changes, not only for the novel's core characters, but also for their entire society. In this manner, Palmer uses his novel and the dilemmas his characters face to call attention to cultural anxieties about technology and how it impacts individuals and society-at-large in the 21st century. Certainly, in *Version Control*, technology, for better *and* worse, makes both Philip and Rebecca Wright who they are. For Philip Wright, his entire professional career—which is at the core of his identity—has to do with his relationship with technology and, specifically relates to the "causality violation device" he invents. For his wife Rebecca, the technology her husband creates is the source of much tension, but it is also ultimately the key to her self-awareness since it both reflects and reveals facets of herself. Moreover, it eventually allows her to save the lives of both her husband and her son. Nonetheless, because she must sacrifice her own life to protect her loved ones, the novel represents new technologies as coming at a high cost.

Through the fictional scenarios that Palmer represents, *Version Control* succeeds in also calling attention to the fact that technology provides innovative ways to reinvent ourselves, but nonetheless places great demands upon us. This is shown by the way that Rebecca Wright and other of the novel's characters change in response to their relationship with technology. Thus, Palmer dramatizes a tension and reality of contemporary life, one which results in widespread cultural ambivalence about what new technologies represent for us now and what they might mean in the future.

6. Clones (and Crime) in Space: Mur Lafferty's *Six Wakes*

American science fiction author Mur Lafferty was born in 1973 and is based in Durham, North Carolina. Her science fiction novel *Six Wakes* (2017) is a murder mystery which takes place aboard the interstellar spacecraft, *The Dormire*, and its plot centers on the ship's crew, a group of clones. The crew is relocating themselves and their cargo (other clones who have been placed in stasis), to an extraterrestrial colony to escape Earth, which, in Lafferty's fictional world, has been devastated by climate change and wars. Similar to Ishiguro's *Never Let Me Go*, *Six Wakes* is a clone narrative and it therefore addresses the ethics of cloning—but it also discusses issues such as identity, individuality, and agency, already fraught notions with get even further complicated because in *Six Wakes*, clones must wrestle with the latent memories of their previous incarnations. Mur Lafferty envisions a future where technology permits "mind-mapping," so new copies of individuals are not only genetically identical but they also retain some of the memories of the experiences of the earlier cloned versions of themselves.

Indeed, while the novel considers both issues related to autonomy and the ethics of cloning, it further complicates these debates by having clones retain the memories of their previous lives; because of this detail, the novel thus also considers the relationship between memory and identity (this question also surfaces in the film *Oblivion*, another clone narrative discussed in this book). The themes of both memory and identity get introduced early on, in the novel's opening pages, when the entire crew of *The Dormire* awakens to a bloody scene. They are in a room with murdered corpses, other versions of themselves. While the clones who comprise the ship's crew ascertain that poisoning, stabbing, and suicide are their apparent causes of death, none of them have memories of what has transpired; therefore, they do not know which of them is responsible for the mayhem aboard *The Dormire*. Moreover, they soon thereafter realize that the bodies look much older than they should, cluing them in to the fact that many years of their memories have been wiped out, as well. Thus begins *Six Wakes*, a closed-circle mystery that take place in outer space.

As these plot details suggest, Lafferty's *Six Wakes* is a novel that relies upon the existence of many clones to engage with the relationship between memory and identity. The novel, however, also raises provocative questions about the ethics of immortality, as well, due to the fact that many of the clones featured are now hundreds of years old and their consciousness could conceivably live on forever. Moreover, Lafferty imagines cloning's legal consequences and thus dramatically renders many of the legal implications that come along with the creation of beings such as clones.

Her novel, for example, goes into great detail about legislation related to cloning and also addresses the legal rights of clones. These details, which operate as part of Lafferty's "world-building," also make manifest the types of concerns that new forms of technology invariably bring about. By bringing to the forefront question such as these, *Six Wakes*, like many of the other novels addressed in this book, pushes readers to contemplate the nature of identity and how it is influenced by our relationship with emerging technologies.

Genre Matters

While these concerns take center stage in *Six Wakes*, Lafferty's novel is also remarkable for the way that she blurs and blends different literary genres as part of her storytelling. Lafferty's novel fits into the science fiction genre in many respects. She relies upon a futuristic science fiction setting since the book takes place during the 25th century; also, like many texts in the science fiction genre, the novel's action occurs aboard a starship. Moreover, its premise, that human cloning has advanced to the point that it is possible to download an individual's consciousness into an artificially created body, is undoubtedly the stuff of science fiction.

Within science fiction, the novel clearly follows the tradition of the clone narrative, a subset of the genre. As Jes Battis underscores, the clone narrative is a "tried-and-true stereotype of SF genre," which tends to involve a "crisis of origins" (97). Indeed, in *Six Wakes*, much like in *Never Let Me Go*, the existence of cloned beings works to call into question traditional notions of the self. In this respect, Lafferty's novel follows popular representations of cloning in science fiction, which "challenge the Western conception of a separate and coherent self and the derived conceptions of moral agency and moral responsibility," a point that Amit Marcus emphasizes in his discussion of clones narratives (389). To be sure, *Six Wakes* portrays clones in a manner reminiscent of other works of the clone narrative sub-genre. In his article "Giving Form to Life: Cloning and Narrative Expectations of the Human," Mark Jerng explains how "fictional narratives of human cloning often represent clones as somewhere between singular individuals and a threatening mass of aggregate, manifesting anxieties around clones as de-individualized persons" (*Jerng* 369). This is, indeed, the case in the novel *Six Wakes* since the clones that make up the ship's crew exist in a liminal space—they do not come really across as autonomous individuals, but neither do they seem like a threatening hoard.

Though *Six Wakes* bears many of the hallmarks of science fiction, Lafferty also relies upon traits common to crime fiction, primarily to set up the mystery which she uses to propel the novel's plot and to establish mood and a sense of urgency. To be sure, critics and reviewers of the novel have tended to label it not only as science fiction, but also as a murder mystery, and, quite specifically, a closed circle mystery, since the setting precludes any so-called outsiders from playing a direct role in the murders that set the stage for the mystery that ensues. For example, in his review of the novel, Robert Bedford describes *Six Wakes* as both an "engaging thriller" and a "locked room murder mystery." He further notes how "clones aboard a generational starship and murder combine" to form the plot of the novel (Bedford). Jason Heller also comments on how the novel operates as "murder mystery," observing how *Six Wakes* "shifts from *whodunit* to *howdunit* to *whydunit* with a breathless sense of escalation."

Not only does Lafferty rely upon traits common to science fiction and crime fiction to propel the plot of *Six Wakes*, but she also borrows heavily from the genre of confessional literature. This comes across especially in the way she constructs multiple narrative viewpoints (these emerge through the book's shifting narrative perspectives) which tend toward the confessional, especially when the book's various narrators (members of the ship's crew) divulge their backstories. As it has traditionally been understood, confessional writing represents a form of un-masking. According to Elke D'Hoker, who makes this point in the essay "Confession and Atonement in Contemporary Fiction," there is, in fact, an "unwritten law of confession" stipulating that the narrator "should not merely reproduce his or her public image but invite the reader behind the facade to glimpse the real person crouching there" (32). What D'Hoker describes here can be seen in the Lafferty's novel since the various narrators reveal previously unknown, and oftentimes secretive, details about their lives, thus confessing their secrets to readers.

Certainly, when un-masking takes place in a work of crime fiction (a genre Lafferty is clearly borrowing from since *Six Wakes* is also a murder mystery), it ties confession in a literary sense with confession in a legal sense. Hence, there is a merging of discourses since, as Peter Brooks highlights in "Storytelling without Fear? Confession in Law and Literature," there is a connection "between legal and literary discourses on the nature and contexts of the confessional act" (115). In the case of *Six Wakes*, this relationship proves to be important, since the book is not just about solving a crime (the murders that propels the novel's initial mystery), but it is also about the legal status of a group of individuals whose culpability in the crime that opens the book's mystery—not to mention all that is transpiring aboard the spacecraft—is mitigated by the fact that their memories have been deliberately tampered with.

The use of the confessional voice is a technique which subverts traditional literary genres, so Lafferty's reliance on it in her storytelling proves significant for this reason, as well. As Mary Beth Harrod explains in *Making Confessions: The Confessional Voice Found Among Literary Genres*, "while the lines of literary conventions separate genres, confessional writing tends to blur those lines by bringing the message of the work to the forefront" (i). Moreover, oftentimes it is the case that a "piece of literature said to be of a particular genre is challenged when one discovers a confessional voice, as it weaves itself among genres and changes the face of the genre itself" (Harrod i). The dynamic that Harrod describes here can be seen in *Six Wakes*, since Lafferty's use of the confessional voice disrupts the traditions of both science fiction and crime fiction. Indeed, in *Six Wakes*, Lafferty blurs and blends different genres to the point that by novel's end, it becomes clear that she has turned the typical clone narrative on its side, thus revealing that she can stretch genre to suit her purposes.

The Ethics of Immortality

Not only does Lafferty borrow from different genres and literary traditions in *Six Wakes*, but she also relies on a trope that can be seen elsewhere within the genre of science fiction. Her clones have the ability to download their consciousness due to a technology she describes as "mind-mapping"; this technology is not unique to *Six Wakes*. Indeed, various science fiction texts, and most notably perhaps, the re-imagined version of *Battlestar Galactica* (2004–2009), features a similar technology (the television series *Battlestar Galactica* is discussed in the second section of this book and, notably, Lafferty herself has written about that series in her 2006 essay "Men Are from Aquaria, Women Are from Caprica").

Lafferty's inclusion of this particular technology is noteworthy, not only because it demonstrates her use of a popular science fiction trope, but also because it brings questions related to immortality into debate. The clones represented in *Six Wakes* are capable of resurrection and thus have the potential to achieve immortality since their consciousness can be downloaded time and again into new cloned bodies. This feature of their existence makes them superior to humans in a sense, but it also works to further separate these clones from human beings. To be sure, mortality is an essential component of human nature.

Fictional representations of human clones, however, in contrast to human beings, have frequently been associated with the pursuit of immortality, a point that Jean Baudrillard highlights in *Screened Out*, where he speaks of clones' potential to stop "the inalienable death of every individual being" (196). Elaine Dewar echoes this sentiment in *The Second Tree: Of Clones, Chimeras and Quests for Immortality*, where she notes that "making clones" has to do with "questing after immortality."

Yet, in *Six Wakes* Lafferty's clones have not fully achieved immortality, though they have gained something akin to it. It *is* possible to kill them—for instance, this could be accomplished by destroying their "mindmaps" or even perhaps by simply choosing not to resurrect a new version once an old one has died (possibilities which get mentioned in the novel). Thus, the clones featured in the novel are figures who occupy liminal spaces—they exist in the space between human and post-human and also occupy a space between life and death—thereby challenging the very nature of these boundaries which they transgress.

There exist complex ethical issues tied to the promise of immortality, as well. In Lafferty's novel, these get dramatically played out since her clones do not really die. Even when they fall victim to foul play, these would-be victims are "reborn" soon after dying since, in Lafferty's imagined future, "clones can regenerate upon death" (Bedford). This facet of their existence speaks to the potential associated with this type of biomedical advancement.

Indeed, the wish to defeat death is a "basic motivation for cloning in many clone narratives" (Marcus 380). However, their near-immortality also raises troubling questions related to bioethics. Should there be limits placed on technologies such as human cloning? Should medical science be governed by what we *can* do or what we *should* do? The many problems and pitfalls associated with the pursuit of immortality also tie into the fact that the practice of resurrecting clones sets them even further apart from humans. Indeed, the practice is arguably de-humanizing.

By pushing these boundaries, Lafferty's clones introduce a new set of concerns to *Six Wakes*, a clone narrative which illustrates how contemporary representations of doubling speak to 21st century anxieties. As Maria Aline Seabra Ferreira explains, contemporary concerns are often bound together with representations of clones, such as our "contemporary fascination with duplication, duality, resemblance, and immortality" (34). These issues, according to Ferreira, "can be said to be the millennial equivalent to the romantic attraction to the double, the dual, [and] the alter ego" (34).

Indeed, the manner in which these beings challenge conventional views about mortality illustrate how messy ontological categories can get. To be sure, in *Six Wakes*, clones not only complicate the binaries between life/death and human/post-human, but they also trouble the dichotomies of man/machine, and thinking/programming—particularly in the sense that their memories can be hacked.

The Role of Memory

Thus, the clones in *Six Wakes* who have attained something akin to an immortal existence, also pose a threat—to others, but to themselves, as well—since they can be re-wired, so to speak, and therefore forced to carry out nefarious tasks. Indeed, as it turns out in *Six Wakes*, "each of these clones has secrets that not even they are fully aware of" (Heller). Readers, in fact, come to learn that these clones cannot fully trust their own memories. For one, the clones are susceptible to losing their memories if they were to die without having a current "mindmap" (which would means that they would be resurrected without their complete memories intact).

This scenario, in fact, is what gets presented at the very beginning of the novel when all of the clones awaken in new bodies and seem to have memories that are a generation out of date (indeed, even the killer him- or herself is unaware of who is responsible for the murders that open the novel). Only making matters worse, there are no surviving records of what happened in the days prior to the clones' collective memory loss. Readers soon learn that their memories are, in fact, subject to hacking and that their minds are also susceptible to other forms of external manipulation. With these types of frightening possibilities presented, the door is left wide open for less-than-scrupulous individuals to try to exploit the clones for their own purposes. Scenarios such as these indeed get played out in the novel, most notably in the cases of two members of the ship's crew, Maria Arenas and Akihiro "Hiro" Sato.

Readers learn that Maria Arenas, prior to boarding *The Dormire*, had been the victim of repeated abductions. During her periods of captivity, she was tortured and forced to hack into both her own and other clones' personalities, only to then be killed and have her memory wiped (so, for a long while she did not realize what had been happening to her). Hiro Sato was also the victim of tampering. He had "yadokari," something akin to multiple personalities, planted within his mind, so he comes across a loose cannon at times and some of his motives are unclear—not only to readers but to himself, as well. Both the case of Maria Arenas and the situation of Hiro Sato bring to the forefront questions about the relationship between memory and identity. Indeed, what makes these concerns even more difficult to discuss is that, in these instances, the clones' memories have been manipulated so any attendant issues related to these characters' guilt, loyalties, or motivation, for example, get similarly portrayed in the novel as complicated.

Going back at least as far as to the time of John Locke (1632–1704), the English philosopher who argued that our memories of our past are part of what gives us a sense of identity, the concept of identity has been tied to memory. Locke, who discusses these concerns in *An Essay Concerning Human Understanding* (1689), holds that personal identity is a matter of psychological continuity. He considered personal identity, or the self, to be founded on consciousness (memory), and not on the substance of either the soul or the body. Since the time when Locke wrote about the relationship between memory and the sense of self, more contemporary "psychological continuity theorists" have tried to update Locke's views (Schechtman 9). As Marya Schechtman explains in her 2005 article "Personal Identity and the Past," psychological continuity theorists understand memory as adding to the constitution of identity "brick by brick," so that each individual memory adds a bit more connection until there is enough to say there is "sameness" (9).

Certainly, even in the 21st century, the popular belief remains that memories create this feeling of "sameness" and, consequently, memory is still believed to play a significant role in forming personal identity. As part of their discussion in the article "Memory and the Sense of Personal Identity," Stanley B. Klein and Shaun Nichols describe how our memories of past episodes provide us with a sense of personal identity or, as they explain it, the sense that "I am the same person as someone in the past" (677). As Klein and Nichols emphasize, not only is memory is "at the heart of the way most people think about personal identity," but it "also is at the heart of philosophical discussions of personal identity," since "memories of past actions go towards constituting personal identity" (678).

In Lafferty's *Six Wakes*, questions of identity and autonomy get presented as rather complicated, especially with respect to the situations like the characters Maria Arenas and Hiro Sato find themselves in, with memories being both stolen from and planted in their minds. Thus, the book dramatically brings to life a tension related to emerging technologies: the fear that our tools can be used to strip individuals of our identity.

To be sure, in *Six Wakes*, this tension gets depicted in the various scenarios which show that it is possible to tamper with memories. Along with this concern come questions related to these characters' roles in the events which unfold in the novel since their actions—and therefore their guilt/culpability—must be understood in the context of them operating with diminished memories. This dilemma is presented as an even further troubling one in the novel since the ontological status of cloned beings like Maria Arenas and Hiro Sato is already very much up for debate.

"World Building" and the Legal Status of the Clones

In *Six Wakes*, Lafferty devotes a significant amount of care to mapping out the legal considerations and consequences that human cloning invariably bring about. This facet of her novel works to raise questions about the ethics of cloning as well as about the legal and ontological status of clones. At the same time, the fact that Lafferty takes time to not only spell out, but to fully flesh out, the legal status of clones in the fictional world she creates demonstrates her "world building."

More than just a framing device, "world building" describes the process of constructing an imaginary world, one often associated with the creation of an entire fictional universe (the term "world building" first appeared in in 1820 in the *Edinburgh Review*; in 1920, the term was used in Arthur Stanley Eddington's *Space Time and Gravitation: An Outline of the General Relativity Theory* to describe the process of imagining hypothetical worlds). In keeping with this practice, Lafferty's imagined futuristic world is replete with details. Indeed, though the novel's action centers on the six crew members aboard *The Dormire*, Lafferty has created a whole world populated by clones and humans alike. As Heller notes, in *Six Wakes*, Lafferty depicts a fully rendered 25th century, with Earth "wracked by climate change," and its populations fighting "wars over dwindling water, and clone uprisings." Lafferty also richly portrays the history behind, and ethical battles over, human cloning.

To be sure, in her fictional world, clones have a rich history as beings—and they also have attained special legal status. For example, unlike humans, in Lafferty's *Six Wakes* clones can designate themselves as their own legal heirs (and beneficiaries), and can thus leave property, money, and other assets to future cloned versions of themselves. There are also, however, special laws that govern their existence. As Heller describes it, "*Six Wakes* is prefaced by a list of seven laws governing the existence of clones, established in the year 2282."

Lafferty, who refers to this collective legislation as "International Law Regarding the Codicils to Govern the Existence of Clones," delineates rules such as "it is unlawful to create more than one clone of a person at a time," "it is unlawful for a clone to bear or father children," and "it is unlawful to put a mindmap onto a body that does not bear the original DNA" (1). These laws specify that "clones must always have the most recent mindmap of their consciousness on a drive on their person" and they mandate that "mindmaps are subject to search by authorities at all times" (Lafferty 1). These codicils make it "unlawful to modify any DNA or mindmap of a clone" (with enforced sterilization being the only exception) and also forbid clones from committing suicide except for in the case of medically-approved euthanasia (Lafferty 1). The legislation goes as far as to mandate the way to dispose of clone's corpse (traditional human funerals, for example, are not allowed). Heller contends that these laws are "reminiscent of Isaac Asimov's famous 'Three Laws of Robotics,'" and, like "Asimov's work, *Six Wakes* offers a set of science-fictional rules that, of course, are going to be bent, broken, and tested throughout the story" (Heller).

Indeed, as the novel progresses, it becomes clear that humans and clones alike break these rules, sometimes with reckless disregard. Maria Arenas, for example, has dealings with unscrupulous humans who freely violate these codicils, in particular by manipulating clones' memories and altering both clones' mindmaps, and, in some cases, their very DNA. This same group also forces her to carry out illegal modifications on other clones and even, at one point, to make her tweak her own mind-map.

Moreover, it also becomes clear that, in certain instances at least, there arise ethical dilemmas related to the codicils that the original legislators may not have fully considered. One such occurrence takes place aboard the ship where there are two cloned versions of Maria Arenas. Though one Maria is comatose (having suffered life-threatening injuries), she is still technically alive—and thus there is a violation of the codicils as they are spelled out. Euthanizing the comatose Maria would fix the breach, but keeping this version of Maria alive might give her the chance, if she were ever to wake up, to divulge what she knows about what transpired onboard the ship. Thus, she might hold the key to the mystery that everyone aboard the ship desperately wants solved. To be sure, throughout Lafferty's *Six Wakes*, ethical dilemmas such as these abound.

Cloning and Controversy

Beyond creating fictional legislation, which her characters test and push to the limits (a feature which underscores the many ethical dilemmas that the novel's characters themselves face), Lafferty also shines a light on contemporary controversies through her fictional scenarios. Thus, she uses her novel to engage readers in current debates. From raising questions about the definition of the individual to probing the nature of identity—and further complicating these concerns because of their relationship with memory—Lafferty considers how these notions are being challenged, contested, and redefined in contemporary times.

Indeed, the novel's depiction of cloned beings presents a 21st century spin on the figure of the double and thus brings forth timely questions about bioethics and the limits of technology. Mur Lafferty's representations of 21st century literary doppelgangers also shows how, in recent years, controversies about identify have frequently merged with debates about technology. Rather than posing these concerns abstractly, in *Six Wakes* Lafferty ties these dilemmas to the plot of her science fiction murder mystery. The result is that readers can ponder scenarios as they dramatically play out in this novel as a way to consider and ultimately process the many contemporary cultural anxieties that new and emerging technologies provoke.

Section II.
Television and Film

"How can we be multiple and coherent at the same time?"—Sherry Turkle, *Life on the Screen: Identity in the Age of the Internet*

Since the time she first posed this question, the line of inquiry that Sherry Turkle introduced about the anxiety and promise of multiplicity has taken different forms as technology and culture have continued to change and evolve. The growing sense that we are all becoming "multiple"—and the fact that we remain ambivalent about it—bear scrutiny because this reflects our fragmented, postmodern state of identity. As a forms of popular culture, 21st century television and film often highlight our culture's hopes and fears. At the same time, they provide lenses through which to view debates about identity, individualism, autonomy, agency, and human rights, a set of concerns that have long-remained important but that have taken on new meanings in the 21st century.

In recent years, there has been an outpouring of storylines in television and film that involve twins or doubles. What accounts for this recent proliferation of doppelgangers (whether twins, clones, or some other form of double) in contemporary film and television? This trend is noteworthy because it points to the enduring significance of the doppelganger, while also showing how the figure can adapt to changing times and shifting cultural values. Additionally, this trend is significant because it highlights and reflects our cultural preoccupations with identity and individualism, both of which are being challenged at the same time as new spaces and technologies are made available through which we can explore and express identity and our individualism. Following this argument, this section of the book will demonstrate how the concepts of "twinning" and "doubling" gain new meanings in the 21st century television and film, meanings which derives directly from our relationships with new technologies—technologies which function as nothing less than cultural interventions—and, thus, which could not have been conceived of prior to the advent of their invention.

Changing Cultural Norms

Cultural norms shift over time, oftentimes in response to human technological development. As Elaine L. Graham argues, technologies have the potential "to be determinative of human experience" (225). Indeed, in recent years, there has been a growing sense "that humans and machines are increasingly assimilated, that human nature cannot be realized apart from its tools and artefacts (either as objects of fear or as instruments of mastery)" (Graham 229). Thus, as Graham explains, "'humanity' is actually constituted in reflexive interaction—even co-evolution—with tools, environment, and artefacts" (229). In other words, how we see ourselves is inextricably linked with how we interact with our tools and technologies. Consequently, as technologies emerge, adapt, and grow, the ways we define ourselves also change.

Even something as seemingly simple as health (or wellness) tends to be defined quite differently from one generation to the next. As Turkle discusses at length, "every era constructs its own metaphors for psychological well-being" (255). In other words, personality traits that may have held much appeal in decades past may no longer be as socially valued today as they once were.

Since the dawn of the 21st century, scholars and cultural historians have taken these ideas even further as part of their discussion of the relationship between humans and technology. For example, Jonathan Bignell (2000), Timothy Taylor (2010), and those working in the emerging field of Media Archaeology, such as Jussi Parikka, have both built on, and further refined, some of Turkle's theories (which she posited in the 1990s). Moreover, in the time since Turkle published her study, technologies have changed and grown, and consequently, our relationship with technology has shifted (even compared to the time when Turkle was writing).

In order to adapt to these new roles and rapidly advancing technologies, those of us living in the 21st century need to be able to play different parts—indeed, we often pride ourselves on being multifaceted. Alas, for many of us, the 21st century also offers a great deal more opportunities to reinvent ourselves. As Graham emphasizes: "Cyberspace affords a much greater freedom to create new selves" (191). Human engagement with technology promises new freedoms and potentials, yet there are myriad complexities to consider, as well.

The Relationship with Technology

The relationship between humans and technology is one fraught with a range of challenges, possibilities, and even potential problems, in part because as we develop and create new technologies, those same tools have the power to change us—in good ways and bad. To be sure, using various forms of technology to try on different identities offers far more than entertainment value. This freedom is fundamentally altering how we see ourselves because the technology we use is working to change us as human beings, just as we change technology.

It is hardly a radical idea that this is one potential effect of technology; indeed, both Donna Haraway and Bruno Latour make detailed cases for the way human beings have been co-evolving—and continue to co-evolve—with our technology. As Graham notes, "we have always been mixed up, co-evolving with our tools, living a hybrid presence," and "the rapid intensification of new technologies over the past fifty years" has simply worked to "accentuate this realization" (228). Timothy Taylor pushes this argument even further in his book *The Artificial Ape: How Technology Changed the Course of Human Evolution*, where he claims that "we did not somehow naturally become smart enough to invent the technology on which we critically rely and that has removed us from the effects of natural selection. Instead, the technology evolved us" (9).

New media theorist Jussi Parikka, who also addresses the entanglement of technology and culture, makes a similar contention in his 2012 book *What Is Media Archaeology?* Parikka focuses on the connection between technology and other discourses, pointing out that "technology does not just determine arts, science does not just determine technology, and art is not only creation and contemplation of beauty. They all work in a co-determining network of historical relations" (69). As part of this intertwined network, recent technological developments have altered—and continue to effect—different discourses as well as how we see ourselves.

Despite its promise, becoming "multiple" can also create tension. This is precisely the concern addressed—and being responded to—through the recent proliferation of doppelgangers in contemporary television and film. Television shows which feature doubles highlight the enduring significance of identity in a fragmented world. The same is true for recent films which consider questions related to identity and reflect our ambivalence about multiplicity.

21st Century Television and Film

The cultural tension related to identity gets examined in this section of the book, which appraises a number of contemporary films and television shows which feature doppelgangers. Chapter 7, "The Twin Formula in *Ringer* and *The Lying Game*," addresses how two contemporary television dramas rework a formula that was popular in the 20th century. Two examples of 21st century science fiction television are the subject of Chapter 8, which is entitled "The Motif of the Double in *Fringe* and *Battlestar Galactica*." This chapter addresses representations of doubles that come about through the plot device of parallel universes (in *Fringe*) and the existence of sentient AI (in the case of *BSG*). *Westworld*, the HBO series about sentient AI who populate a theme park, is the subject of Chapter 9. Although *Westworld* engages with a number of issues related to the ethics of creating AI, the show also offers an interesting treatment of the double through the character Bernard Lowe (who is made in the image of the park's co-founder, Arnold Weber).

Chapter 10 offers an analysis BBC America's *Orphan Black*, a science fiction television series that follows the pattern of the clone narrative. As its subject, this chapter considers the many cultural anxieties related to cloning, as well as the myriad identity- and human rights-related questions that discussions of cloning inevitably raise, that get reflected in the television show, *Orphan Black*. While Chapter 11, "Cinematic Clones in *The Island* and *Oblivion*," considers the issue of cloning, as well, the focus here is on the ethics of cloning. By looking at two recent films, both of which are clone narratives about individuals who are, at first, unaware of their nature, and then, only later, come to realize that they are actually clones created for dubious purposes, the chapter calls attention to the way these texts further problematize an already controversial subject.

The last chapter in this section is "Monstrous Doubling and Magical Illusion in *The Prestige*." It examines a film that includes both twins and clones as part of its plot. The film follows rival magicians, one of whom is actually a twin and the other of whom has found a way to clone himself. The film's treatment of the doppelganger theme highlights the fear associated with becoming multiple while also addressing anxieties related to emerging technologies.

Representing Transformation and Tension on Screen

What this grouping of films and television shows share in common is that, in each, a single actor portrays multiple characters, in essence, impersonating different people and trying out different lives and identities. They all reflect the sense that identity is becoming increasing fractured in postmodern times. Together, these films and television shows, through their storylines involving doubles, reflect the tension that so many of us living in the 21st century feel about becoming "multiple," as well as the complexities that new technologies bring along with them.

There is, to be sure, as Parikka and others have outlined, a complicated relationship between technology and other discourses (including popular culture). This dynamic reveals itself in the exhaustive list of contemporary storylines that involve twins, doubles, clones, and doppelgangers because the popularity of these tropes remain linked to the many recent technological developments which enable members of our society to try on different identities. Indeed, in many ways, these technologies have altered—and continue to effect—how we see ourselves.

While it is true that some welcome the transformative abilities of this type of technology, there are others for whom it is the root of much anxiety, one born out of the fear that there "is no 'self' behind the expressions and performances of identity" (Graham 193). The tension alluded to by Graham is precisely what storylines address by featuring the repeated motifs of twins, doubles, and doppelgangers. A closer examination of examples from 21st century television and film will illustrate this contention.

7. The Twin Formula in *Ringer* and *The Lying Game*

Storylines involving twin sisters became "standard fare in 20th century film and television," a point that Juliana de Nooy makes in *Twins in Contemporary Literature and Culture*, a 2005 book which explores the phenomenon (50). Many of these plots conformed to what is now known as the "good twin/bad twin" formula, a pattern characterized by positioning an innocent young woman against her worldlier twin sister (a variation of this formula can be seen in Audrey Niffenegger's 2009 novel, *Her Fearful Symmetry*, which is the focus of an early chapter in this book). Offering an update on this formula, two television dramas, *Ringer* and *The Lying Game*, debuted during the fall 2011 season. Both shows feature sets of identical twin sisters, each set portrayed by one actress. In both series, the sister in the seemingly less fortunate situation steps in to her twin's life and is then forced to navigate a series of precarious situations in order to "pass" as her twin—while doing so, each unearths myriad mysteries in her twin sister's life.

Starring Sarah Michelle Gellar, who plays twin sisters Bridget Kelly and Siobhan Martin, *Ringer* is an American television series that premiered on The CW on September 13, 2011. *The Lying Game* is an American teen drama television series produced by Alloy Entertainment and Warner Horizon Television for ABC Family. The lead actress in the series is Alexandra Chando, who plays twin sisters Sutton Mercer and Emma Becker. *The Lying Game*, which is based on a series of novels by Sara Shepard, debuted on August 15, 2011. While *The Lying Game* targets a younger demographic (in terms of viewership) than *Ringer*, both shows belong to the genre of the television drama.

The television series *Ringer* follows identical twin sisters Bridget Kelly and Siobhan Martin. Bridget Kelly is a recovering drug addict who makes a living as an exotic dancer in Wyoming. Bridget initially agreed to testify against her employer, an organized crime boss named Bodaway Macawi (played by Zahn McClarnon), a man she witnessed commit murder, but she changes her mind. She fears that FBI Agent Victor Machado (played by Nestor Carbonell), who convinced her to testify, cannot protect her from Macawi, who has already murdered several other witnesses. Because of this situation, Bridget runs to New York and meets up with her estranged twin sister, Siobhan Martin, but, soon after Bridget arrives in New York, Siobhan, who had kept her twin's existence secret from her husband and friends, mysteriously disappears when the two go out on a boat (Bridget mistakenly believes that Siobhan has committed suicide by jumping into the ocean; she does not learn until the Season 1 finale that her sister is actually still alive). After Siobhan's apparent suicide, Bridget assumes her sister's identity and tries to fit in among Siobhan's affluent Manhattan social circle.

The television drama *The Lying Game* centers on Emma Becker, a good-natured teenager who had been living with a foster family until she discovers that she has an identical twin sister named Sutton Mercer (played by the same actor). The twin girls were separated at birth, with Sutton being adopted by wealthy parents and living a seemingly perfect life. Sutton convinces Emma to step into her life for a few days so she can learn about their birth mother in Los Angeles. Days turn into many weeks and Emma realizes that Sutton has secrets of her own to hide.

Complicating the Twin Formula in Contemporary Television

As the above descriptions suggest, the television dramas *Ringer* and *The Lying Game* have much in common. Both feature plots driven by slowly unraveling mysteries about crime, deception, betrayal, and family drama. Another similarity that they share is that both programs contain sets good and bad twins. Indeed, as popular television series that feature doubles, both *Ringer* and *The Lying Game* present—and then eventually complicate—the binaries of both the good twin/bad twin and the rich twin/poor twin formulas, and, in this respect, they also follow a long tradition of cinematic noir (and they also hearken back to the formula seen in *Her Fearful Symmetry*, since that novel also complicates the good twin/bad twin formula).

As Linda Ruth Williams illustrates in her book *The Erotic Thriller in*

Contemporary Cinema, there are a number of 20th century noir films that include sets of "good and bad twins" (32). Indeed, as she is quick to point out, the "twins scenario is a common pairing for women in cinematic and literary noir" (Williams 354). Charles Derry makes a similar contention is his book *The Suspense Thriller: Films in the Shadow of Alfred Hitchcock*, where he addresses twins in the context of "the doubling so common to the suspense thriller" (Derry 210).

The specific pattern described by Williams is further reflected in the plots of the television series *Ringer* and *The Lying Game* because many of the examples that she discusses in her book involve plots revolving around a "bad twin's (faked) death," which results in the "good twin" questioning "her own identity," a formula which *Ringer* closely follows—and a pattern from which *The Lying Game* borrows certain elements (32). As part of her discussion of scenarios played out in various 20th century noir films, Williams argues that "this is a doubling which liberates, whereby one woman might fetishistically shadow her mirror-image" (21). Indeed, a similar argument could well be made about the function of doubles in *Ringer* and *The Lying Game*, for in each drama the twin emerging from hard times finds a certain degree of liberation by impersonating her twin sister.

Like many of the plots of older noir films, *Ringer* and *The Lying Game* pose longstanding questions. To what degree are we defined by our choices? How do our life experiences shape us? What role does our environment play in shaping our lives? In *The Lying Game*, for instance, we witness the high cost of the many secrets and lies that surround Sutton, while we see how her twin sister Emma, despite her more difficult upbringing, maintains a more positive outlook and better relationships (compared to Sutton). In *Ringer*, we can see Siobhan's desire for vengeance against a sister who she holds responsible for the tragic death of her young son, Sean, at the same time as we learn how Bridget's guilt over this same tragedy has driven her to abuse alcohol and drugs. Thus, to an extent, these series follow in the trend that scholars like Linda Ruth Williams describe.

Yet, for all of the similarities these television shows share with 20th century representations of the good twin/bad twin and rich twin/poor twin formulas, the recent permutations of the twin plot that can be seen in *Ringer* and *The Lying Game* diverge from this tradition in significant ways. *Ringer* and *The Lying Game* make us consider such timely questions as: How flexible are we? Can we change and adapt to today's world? And, to what extent are we the authors of our own lives? The fact that *Ringer* and *The Lying Game* confront questions such as these as part of their storylines suggests that there is new cultural significance with respect to representations of 21st century twins. In our era, being able to survive—let alone to thrive—depends on our ability to adapt, change, and remain flexible.

Dramatic Renderings of Identity in 21st Century Television

In *Ringer* and *The Lying Game*, both Bridget Kelly and Emma Becker clearly possess these traits in abundance. They adapt to their new situations so well that they are able to successfully "pass" as their twins, convincing family, friends, and romantic partners alike that they are people who they are not. The fact that both Bridget and Emma so easily step into their twin sisters' lives paints identity as fluid and negotiable, rather than as something fixed and permanent. Moreover, both Bridget and Emma are able to achieve newfound happiness in their new roles—this speaks to the promise and potential of multiplicity. Namely, Emma appreciates Sutton's parents, sister Laurel, friends, and secret boyfriend Ethan in ways that Sutton never did since Sutton refused to publicly acknowledge Ethan Whitehorse as her boyfriend because of his social class and less-than-desirable (in Sutton's opinion, at least) background and because he has had run-ins with the law. Similarly, in *Ringer*, Bridget falls in love with Siobhan's estranged husband Andrew and makes amends with her "new" stepdaughter, his daughter Juliet (a girl with whom Siobhan was constantly at odds).

Yet, alongside the many benefits associated with multiplicity that these television shows display, *Ringer* and *The Lying Game* also address the many challenges and potential problems that go along with being multiple in the 21st century. Though Bridget and Emma both seem happier in their new roles, the two nonetheless remain pursued by danger. In both series, mistaken identities lead to not only confusion, but also to threats and peril. These problems become visible as the twins in *Ringer* and *The Lying Game* are plagued by stalkers, witness crimes, suffer a car accident, and are threatened with repeated attempts on their lives, among other dangers. Thus, by showing the dangers associated with becoming multiple, the anxieties we have about—as well as the potentially negative consequences of—multiplicity come to light.

In a number of ways, the rich twin/poor twin formula takes on a very different tenor in *Ringer* and *The Lying Game* precisely because these television shows are complicated by 21st century problems such as a Ponzi scheme (in *Ringer*), organized crime and drug trade (in *Ringer*), and high dollar medical malpractice suits (in *The Lying Game*). Reminders of the (relatively recent) real estate crisis and the economic recession that plagued the first decade of the 2000s can be found, as well. For example, in *The Lying Game*, a teenage boy is found to be squatting in a foreclosed home. When Laurel Mercer (Sutton's sister) learns that her new boyfriend Justin doesn't live at the address he provided the school, she grows suspicious. After doing some digging, she discovers that he is actually an orphan who has been "squatting" in an otherwise unoccupied house (these events occur in the episode "Bad Boys Break Hearts," which is Episode 6 of Season 1). This type of inclusion makes the show's plot timely and highlights the type of common but newsworthy real-estate related challenges of the early years of the new millennium.

Similarly, *Ringer* also points to the types of stories that could frequently be found on the nightly news during the first decade of the new millennium. For instance, in *Ringer*, there is a complicated blackmail scenario (which is economically motivated) and the show's viewers eventually learn that the Martin family affords their lifestyle—and their multiple residences—with ill-begotten monies and through unethical means. Thus, it is worth noting that even when these television series pose an age-old question (such as, how large of a role do our material circumstances play in terms of how we see ourselves and how others see us?), the question is presented in the context of 21st century concerns. The combined result is that both *Ringer* and *The Lying Game* dramatically portray some of the ways that contemporary representations of twins and doppelgangers are rife with new meanings, meanings which are tied to 21st century debates.

8. The Motif of the Double in *Fringe* and *Battlestar Galactica*

In much the same way that *Ringer* and *The Lying Game* dramatically portray how contemporary representations of doubles are rife with significance, two science fiction television series, *Fringe* (2008–2013) and *Battlestar Galactica* (2004–2009), also illustrate how growing cultural norms and emerging technologies have had an effect on modern-day representations. In *Fringe*, rather than featuring twins, the series concerns two identical looking women who are instead doppelgangers, hailing from parallel universes. The women (both played by Anna Torv) share the same face and are both special agents with the Fringe Division (a special division of the FBI), but otherwise the two possess different traits and they have had divergent lives. In *Battlestar Galactica*, identical looking individuals are actually copies of the same model of human-looking Cylons ("Cylon" stands for Cybernetic Life Form Nodule and describes a race of sentient machines); in the case of Cylons, while the models are identical in appearance, they hold different and sometimes conflicting allegiances, and have had vastly dissimilar life experiences.

In both *Fringe* and *Battlestar Galactica*, there are numerous scenarios that have emerge as part of the series' science fiction plots which demonstrate how growing cultural norms and developing technologies have had an effect on modern-day representations of twins and doubles. The plot twists, themes, and dilemmas that can be found in these series respond directly to the presence of emerging technologies—and, similar to *Ringer* and *The Lying Game*—these science fiction television programs reflect both the promise and the many anxieties associated with the numerous recent technological developments that allow us to explore different identities. To be sure, within the plots of *Fringe* and *Battlestar Galactica*, there resides an awareness of the ways these new technologies have affected—and continue to alter—how we define ourselves. These shows acknowledge the ongoing reconsideration of the more traditional and unitary notions of identity that were once so prevalent. Similar to *Ringer*'s and *The Lying Game*'s treatment of twins, *Fringe* and *Battlestar Galactica* offer a new twist on another old motif: the double.

The double is a popular and recurring motif in science fiction, the significance of which has been explored by scholars and cultural historians alike. In "Secret Sharers: The Doppelgänger Motif in Speculative Fiction," Frank Dietz identifies and defines three stages of the "double" in science fiction: the "mechanical doppelgänger" (mechanical doppelgangers typically refer to robotic counterparts and, according to Dietz, these represent the double in the purest sense), the "allohistorical doppelgänger" (meaning doubles that come about through the existence of parallel worlds or histories), and "wetware" ("wetware" is a popular Cyberpunk term which describes something that is fluid or exchangeable; it represents the dissolution of the self in digital form) (209–210).

Dennis Kogel and Irene Schäfer further expand Dietz' three categories of the figure of the doppelganger—mechanical, allohistorical, and "wetware" (or virtual)—in their essay "The Doppelgänger Motif in Science Fiction Film," where they envision the doppelganger as "five distinct motifs used in film and serial TV (clones, artificial intelligence, time travel, parallel universes, virtual identities)" (126). Kogel and Schäfer aim to show "how the idea of the self is both presented and challenged in contemporary film, how it relates to the challenges and issues of modern capitalism in an information society and what it tells us about the shifting values of human life and identity" (126–127). As the examination that follows reveals, the doubles featured in *Fringe* and *Battlestar Galactica* borrow from, at the same time as they build upon, notions of the doppelganger as it has been described by Dietz and expanded upon by Kogel and Schäfer.

Am I Seeing Double?

The television program *Fringe* follows a woman named Olivia Dunham who works as an FBI Special Agent assigned to the "Fringe Division." Through the plot device of parallel universes, fans of the series learn that Olivia has a double (she is not unique in this regard since certain of the show's other characters also have doubles). Olivia has a photographic memory and maintains a close relationship with her sister Rachel and niece Ella, but she and her sister lost their mother in 1992. In contrast, her double, who prefers to be called Liv (viewers of the series have dubbed her "Alt-Olivia" or "Fauxlivia"), is an Olympic medal winning sharpshooter who remains close to her still-living mother, but who continues to mourn her sister Rachel Dunham, who died in childbirth (Rachel and daughter both die in childbirth of VPE, or Viral Propagated Eclampsia, a disease which does not exist in this universe).

A second, related overarching plot-line links Olivia to a series of illicit medical experiments performed by Dr. Walter Bishop (played by John Noble), another series' regular and present-day colleague of Olivia Dunham. Walter Bishop, along with Massive Dynamic founder William Bell (played by Leonard Nimoy), tested the drug Cortexiphan (a chemical developed by Bell which ostensibly allows children injected with it to retain higher brain functions which would normally deteriorate with age) on Olivia and a number of other child subjects at a daycare facility in Jacksonville, Florida. As a result, Olivia is capable of unspecified psychic abilities. For instance, in Season 1, Olivia shuts off a series of lights wired into a bomb as a kill switch simply by thinking it. Later in the series, it is revealed that, as a child, Olivia started the fire with her mind. Viewers also later learn that has the unique ability to discern if an object originated in the alternate universe (this is due to a "glimmer" that only she can see).

Olivia's doppelganger Liv is also an agent with the Fringe Division, but she possesses different traits than the Olivia of the prime universe (and, significantly, Fauxlivia was not part of the Cortexiphan trials). While Olivia is a serious-minded loner with a photographic memory who dedicates her considerable talents and much of her time to her work, Fauxlivia has a far more carefree personality, not to mention a sense of humor (something prime Olivia seems to lack). Prime Olivia had an abusive stepfather, and shot him several times in defense of her mother and herself (Olivia shot but did not kill him), while no similar back story has been revealed about Fauxlivia. Through Olivia and her doppelganger, *Fringe* raises thought-provoking questions about the degree to which our upbringing, experiences, and environments shape our personalities.

Cultural Anxieties about Multiplicity

The television series, however, also relies on the dynamic present between the two women to explore the many cultural anxieties associated with multiplicity. In numerous episodes of *Fringe*, Olivia comes not only comes face to face with her doppelganger, thereby symbolically confronting another side of herself, but the show suggests that Olivia (deservedly perhaps), at least initially, harbors deep-seeded feelings of resentment for her doppelganger. This stems, in part, from the deception Fauxlivia practices on those close to Olivia including Peter Bishop (prime Olivia's on-again/off-again love interest) who sleeps with and impregnates Fauxlivia (who pretends to be Olivia and seduces him, thus performing a version of the "bed switch trick" that gets discussed in an earlier chapter of this book) in one of the series' timelines. Though the hostility between the two women derives in part from Fauxlivia's attempt to take over Olivia's life, the difficulties between them persist even after those events occur and, even in an alternate timeline (one which has been imagined without the presence of Peter Bishop, who is the source of so much conflict for the two Olivias), there remains considerable friction between the two women. This suggests that another type of anxiety is thus provoked by the two different versions of the same woman coming face-to-face: each represents for the other an imagined alternate existence at the same time as each Olivia showcases for the other her weaknesses. Prime Olivia's single-mindedness regarding her work and independent nature stand in contrast to Fauxlivia's more lighted-hearted and sociable personality, traits which also bespeak Fauxlivia's reliance and dependence on others (at least in comparison to Olivia).

The existence of Olivia's doppelganger also brings to the forefront another anxiety related to multiplicity: the fear of "decentering," which threatens dissolution of self. Just as identity in a cyberworld is fluid and negotiable, for Olivia and Fauxlivia identity proves to be rather unstable, as well, and this operates as a source of conflict in many of the episodes. One such example is an episode entitled "Olivia" (the first episode of Season 3) which opens with Olivia strapped to a chair in a psychiatrist's office. Though this is the Olivia from the prime universe, the doctor is attempting to convince her that she is their universe's Olivia. As the scene continues, we learn that alt-universe's Walter Bishop (also known as "Walternate") has been injecting her with something to give her Fauxlivia's memories to convince her that she is *their* Olivia. A similar dynamic can be witnessed in multiple episodes of Season 4, where Olivia suffers memory loss at the same time as she appears to gain a different Olivia's memories. Rather than presenting this experience as either purely negative or positive, *Fringe* shows Olivia dealing with very ambivalent feelings about her simultaneous gain and loss of memories, thus suggesting ambivalence about the fluidity associated with identity in the 21st century.

Though perhaps the most striking, the case of Olivia and her doppelganger is far from the only example of doubles present in the televisions series. As Sarah Clarke Stuart points out in her recent book *Into the Looking Glass: Exploring the Worlds of Fringe*, an analysis of *Fringe* "reveals the narrative's preoccupation with the double" (Stuart 120). From the program's premise of following a team of "Fringe" agents as they investigate a strange series of occurrences which are related to mysteries surrounding a parallel universe, to the numerous and repeated use of doppelgangers and twins, "*Fringe* employs the archetype of the double in various modes" (Stuart 120–121). Although *Fringe* relies upon archetypal representations of the double—and to an extent, borrows from these traditions—the significance of what doppelgangers represent in *Fringe* moves beyond these traditions in substantial ways. Indeed, in *Fringe*, there are new meanings bound together with the series' portrayal of doubles, meanings which reflect 21st century concerns about identity and multiplicity in a digital age.

As *Fringe* scholars and bloggers alike have been quick to notice, twins are featured in many of the television series' episodes, albeit sometimes as subplots to the series' overarching plots. A notable example can be found in "The Road Not Taken," the nineteenth episode of the first season of *Fringe* (it first aired in the United States on May 5, 2009). "The Road Not Taken" is an episode about "twin sisters endowed with pyrokinetic abilities" who become the subject of the Fringe team's investigation (Stuart 121). Stuart argues that "their presence, which precedes the appearance of the alternate *Fringe* universe, foreshadows the far-reaching doppelgänger effect that occurs once the other universe emerges" (121).

Another noteworthy example is "Amber 31422" (which first aired in the U.S. on November 4, 2010), an episode from Season 3 that set *Fringe* bloggers a flurry. The episode's storyline revolves around a set of identical male twins. One twin is trapped in amber for several years while his brother assumes his identity (according to *Fringe* mythology, "amber" is an advanced substance that begins as a gas and hardens into a solid, mineral-like substance similar in characteristic, color, hardness, and translucency to naturally occurring amber; a person trapped in amber is not killed, but is placed in a state of suspended animation). This dynamic is significant because it presents a new twist on an old formula. Steve Wyble (a blogger and *Yahoo! Voices* contributor) comments on how *Fringe* re-imagines an old plot device in this episode. He explains: It's a concept that has been done before. Just look at *The Parent Trap*, in which twin girls separated at birth meet at summer camp and decide to swap places. Or look at Mark Twain's novel *The Prince and the Pauper*, in which a poor boy switches places with a prince. But *Fringe* nevertheless manages to inject a little originality into the concept by putting it in a science fiction setting" (Wyble). Stuart also discusses this episode of *Fringe*, arguing that "this scenario stands as a clear parallel narrative to Fauxlivia hijacking Olivia's life" (Stuart 121).

Though the episodes "The Road Not Taken" and "Amber 31422" feature plots about twins, as *characters* these two sets of twins play relatively minor roles in the grand scheme of *Fringe* mythology rather than taking center stage (as they do in *Ringer* and *The Lying Game*). Instead, the sets of twins in "The Road Not Taken" and "Amber 31422" primarily work to anticipate the series' larger interest in the doppelganger figure—a figure which is introduced and reintroduced time and time again through the plot device of the existence of parallel universes. In *Fringe*, the repeated use of doppelgangers is the formula upon which so many of the series' elements depend. At the same time, in *Fringe*, it is the doppelganger which serves to underscore how identity in the 21st century is fluid and negotiable.

Fringe justifies the presence of so many doppelgangers—indeed, all of the main characters except Peter Bishop (who is a notable exception because he is actually the double from the parallel universe) not only have living doppelgangers, but they also have occasion to meet them thanks to the plot device of parallel universes, a contrivance which also ties into the series' continued and repeated focus on exploring identity. As Stuart observes, in *Fringe* the "warring of the alternate universes represents the self fighting itself—aggression and repression directed inward. In fiction the double dramatizes the contradictory nature of the self, reflecting the potential that normally lies dormant in each person" (Stuart 121). The existence of the many doppelgangers in *Fringe* opens up a space for the many anxieties and potentials associated with multiplicity to be played out dramatically at the same time as they serve to highlight the emerging importance of multiplicity in the 21st century.

Beyond the dynamic between these two women—which remains central to the television series—the existence of other characters' doppelgangers also prove important to *Fringe*'s overarching concerns. The case of Walter Bishop is particularly compelling, for the existence of his doppelganger ("Walternate") figures significantly into the series' plot and conflicts. The case of the two Walter Bishops also serves to highlight how experiences shape us and how identity, rather than remaining stable and fixed, is rather fluid. In the *Fringe* prime Universe, Dr. Walter Bishop worked out of a laboratory in the basement of the Kresge Building at

Harvard University. He maintained a cover that he did research for a toothpaste company, but in reality, he worked as part of a classified U.S. Army experimental program called Kelvin Genetics, run under the supervision of DARPA (DARPA is the acronym for Defense Advanced Research Projects Agency; in the context of *Fringe*, DARPA is associated with Kelvin Genetics, a classified project sponsored by the U.S. Army). In 1991, Dr. Bishop was institutionalized at St. Claire's Hospital, a mental hospital, after an assistant was killed in his laboratory.

Walternate shares some common history with his counterpart since they both marry the same Elizabeth and, like Walter, he and Elizabeth have an only son named Peter, but there are significant variations in their back stories, as well: William Bell of the alternate universe dies in a car accident as a child and thus never meets Walternate. Walternate, as a result of having been appointed as the United States "National Security Czar," becomes politically powerful. He achieves financial security as a result of having founded a lucrative company called "Bishop Dynamic," which is the parallel to Massive Dynamic, the company founded by William Bell in the prime universe. Walternate goes on to become the U.S. Secretary of Defense, thus becoming wealthier and even more powerful. All the while, his counterpart lives out his days in a mental hospital. The striking differences between the two men's lives demonstrate how choice and chance can potentially play powerful roles in determining our fate. At the same time, the dynamic between the two men reveals identity to be negotiable, rather than fixed.

Similarly, many of the series' other characters, such as Philip Broyles, Lincoln Lee, and Astrid Farnsworth (all of whom work for Fringe Division), showcase how identity in the 21st century is fluid and negotiable through the sometimes subtle ways they diverge from their doppelgangers. For example, prime Philip Broyles (played by Lance Reddick) is divorced while his counterpart (also played by Reddick) remains married. Prime Lincoln Lee (played by Seth Gabel) is bookish and introverted, while his doppelganger (also played by Gabel) is much more confident and extroverted.

The prime version of Astrid Farnsworth (played by Jasika Nicole) makes her living as a Junior FBI Agent assisting Agent Dunham and Dr. Walter Bishop. Personable, empathetic, and easygoing, prime Astrid maintains a close relationship with her father. Her doppelganger (also played by Nicole) is an autistic computer and statistics specialist with Fringe division. Unlike prime Astrid, this version laments not being closer to her father.

Taken together, these characters make evident the complicated nature of identity formation. These characters also demonstrate how human personality traits, rather than being fixed and unchangeable, are malleable and oftentimes constructed as a result of our environments and interactions with others. The fact that so many characters in the series have doppelgangers speaks to *Fringe*'s continued focus on identity and persistent preoccupation with the double, a preoccupation which reflects an awareness of the many manifestations of multiplicity in our culture today.

"There are many copies": The Multiplicity Motif in *Battlestar Galactica*

Like *Fringe*, the science fiction television series *Battlestar Galactica* remains preoccupied with the motif of the double. A 21st century reimagining of a series that originally premiered in the 1970s, *Battlestar Galactica* (2003–2009) raises thought-provoking questions about identity in a digital age. In *BSG*, doubles appear via the plot device of numerous human-looking "Cylon" models ("Cylon" stands for Cybernetic Life Form Nodule), a race of sentient machines. As beings, Cylons raise provocative ontological questions. Indeed, Cylons are both mechanical doppelgangers and cyborgs, and they thus complicate, if not altogether dissolve, the binaries of human/machine, thinking/programming, and natural/artificial—to name just a few. In this sense, as well as in many others, the 2003–2009 *BSG* has a "renewed focus on the fundamental nature of what it means to be human," a point Lincoln Geraghty makes in his book *American Science Fiction Film and Television* (117).

Global Politics and Identity

Beyond the repeated use of the doppelganger figure, which remains a hallmark of the series and is presented as a multilayered and complex formula, there are other recurring themes which situate the television series as timely and prescient. As Mark A. McCutcheon points out in his essay "Downloading Doppelgängers: New Media Anxieties and Transnational Ironies in *Battlestar Galactica*," the incarnation of *BSG* that debuted in 2003 is a product of a globalized 21st century, and a series that could only have been created by a post–9/11 America:

> Premiering as a cable mini-series in 2003, *Battlestar* became a fascinatingly anachronistic and transnational curiosity—a 1978 concept that could only make sense after 9/11—and a pointedly American allegory about disaster, diaspora, and deregulation, that would only be produced with pivotal Canadian resource contributions. It reproduces the premise of the 1978 series, but through a realist aesthetic shared by other post–9/11 action series such as *24* [3].

McCutcheon is not alone in making this contention. Geraghty also notes how *Battlestar Galactica* is full of "allusions to the events of 9/11, America's War on Terror, and the military occupation of Afghanistan and Iraq" (119).

Thus, in addition to provoking anxieties about identity in digital age, the series also probes many of the difficult global political dilemmas we are faced with today. Rather than treating 21st century American conflicts as black-and-white issues, *Battlestar Galactica* instead paints 21st century political debates and military conflict as multifaceted and complex. For example, by reversing roles in terms of the occupier/occupied dynamic, *BSG*, pushes viewers to consider viewpoints other than those espoused by mainstream American media and politicians. The show also complicates the distinctions between hero/traitor and patriot/terrorist. The result is that viewers are forced to reconsider their assumptions about good and evil, a point Geraghty emphasizes in his analysis of the series: "Humans left on occupied New Caprica use guerilla tactics and suicide bombings to attack and kill the Cylons and their human collaborators. Such actions force the audience to momentarily symphathise with those we would normally consider terrorists, our enemies in America's War on Terror, thus problematising our conceptions of right and wrong, civilised and barbaric" (119). The dynamic present between the humans and numerous Cylon models symbolically represents many of the conflicts present in a post–9/11 world. As McCutcheon puts it, the re-imagined Cylons "embody a metonymic chain of enemy figures and security threats: spies, sleeper agents, hackers, 'homegrown' terrorists, the so-called 'clash of civilisations,' and 'synthetic' alien 'skin jobs'" (McCutcheon 7).

In *Battlestar Galactica*, humanoid Cylons are the leaders of the Cylon society and the revelation—made in the re-imagined series' 2003 miniseries (which functioned as the series' pilot)—that they can convincingly mimic human form creates panic among the humans. What further fuels humans' fear of Cylons, as well builds tension and creates conflict in the television program, is that they are capable of many of the same psychological and emotional responses as human beings, and can thus create and maintain interpersonal, emotionally-complex, and even sexual relationships with humans (though the Cylons are able to "pass" as human, they nonetheless have certain abilities which humans do not such as increased stamina, superior physical strength, and the ability to interface with computer systems).

This realization provokes tension because humans come to understand that the Cylon models can effectively "pass" as humans when they choose to, but it also raises difficult questions related human rights: What *are* human rights in a post-human world? Do aliens and others—or in the case of *Battlestar Galactica*, Cylons—have the same inalienable rights that we claim humans do? Through episodes that feature brutal scenes of torture and rape (of Gina, one of the incarnations of Cylon Model Six) and attempted sexual assault (of one of the Cylon Model Eights), to the numerous episodes that include heated discussions about abortion and the reproductive rights of both human and Cylon females, *BSG* also engages in other timely political debates.

Redefining Identity in the 21st Century

Beyond their role of provoking current political debates, the twelve Cylon models function as a means for the series to examine our collective redefining of identity and the reconsideration of individualism that is taking place in our digital age. The humanoid Cylons are a reflection of, even a response to, the many new technologies which make multiplicity available in the 21st century. Multiplicity is associated with flexibility—a much-needed trait in our global economy—but is also creates feelings of insecurity. How are we to know another's motives or intentions? How can we ever know who we are dealing with and what they want from us? As Alison Peirse explains in her essay "Uncanny Cylons: Resurrection and Bodies of Horror," the Cylon models exist as the source of much anxiety for the humans because their identical appearance makes it impossible to tell who is beneath the surface: "*BSG* creates bodily anxieties not through the replication of the double alone, but through the fact that these doubles are identical human in appearance and have independent thought and distinguishable personalities" (126).

Characters such as Cylon Model Eight—whose many copies come to be known as Sharon Valeri, Boomer, and Athena—show just how complicated loyalty is, and how unpredictable alliances can be. As Julie Hu Pegues outlines in her article "Miss Cylon: Empire and Adoption in *Battlestar Galactica*," the series produces anxieties through this character: "the multivalent construction of Boomer are situated within the current moment of globalization, which may be characterized by a 'post–Fordist' or period of 'flexible accumulation'" (Pegues 191). The numerous sleeper agents—Number Eight is originally presented as a sleeper agent (though she comes to realize that she is a Cylon relatively early on in the series), and all of the "Final Five" are sleeper agents—even further provoke these anxieties, for in their case, not only are the human characters left wondering about their true essence, both viewers and, significantly, the characters themselves are forced to consider if there is any true self beneath the surface (again, this is an example of the "decentering" Graham refers to).

Yet, in *Battlestar Galactica*, not only are the cultural anxieties associated with multiplicity provoked through the representation of the multiple copies, but the sense that humans and machines are inextricably linked is also made evident through the existence of the many Cylon models and the humans who interact (and, in one case, breed) with them. A timely television series, *Battlestar Galatica* literalizes the metaphor that human and machine are, for better or worse, irrevocably bound together. In lieu of sexual reproduction, humanoid Cylons have the ability to download their consciousness into another body when the body they are using dies, giving them virtual immortality (at least until the fourth season episode "The Hub," when the humans destroy one of their "resurrection ships"). This realization is even further unsettling for the human characters for, as Peirse illustrates, "while they appear on the surface to be doubles, creating an initial moment of uncanniness, the bodies of the Cylons become horrific when it is realized that they are autonomous and cannot die" (126).

The Cylon ability to resurrect further complicates how the series address identity in a global age. As Peirse explains, the "constant dissolution of identity and the resurrected Cylon body result in a sense of unease for the viewer, and anxiety for both humans and Cylons in the series" (Peirse 121). Taken together, this anxiety along with the characters, scenarios, and conflicts that are all present in *Battlestar Galactica*, reflect the growing sense that human nature cannot be realized apart from its technology and tools.

The Lens of Science Fiction: Addressing Identity, Ethics and Emerging Technologies

As science fiction series that rely on the motif of the double, both *Battlestar Galactica* and *Fringe* illustrate how shifting cultural norms and emerging technologies have had an effect on modern-day representations of the figure. They also highlight the way the figure functions as a cultural vehicle to shine a light on contemporary cultural anxieties. To be sure, both *Battlestar Galactica* and *Fringe* highlight the intersection of identity-related concerns, ethics, and emerging technologies—and they do so by relying on the figure of the doppelganger.

In the case of *Fringe*, the plot-lines frequently pose questions about the limits—ethical as well as other—of science. Discussing the series as a whole, Phil Smolenski and Charlene Elsby argue that "*Fringe* provides us with the opportunity" to consider "abstract questions about the ethical significance of scientific advancement" (114). In many instances, these problems are brought to light through representations of the double. In the case of *Battlestar Galactica*, the series relies on the trope of the double and how it has historically represented the uncanny, but also raises difficult but timely questions about human rights by addressing controversies ranging from torture and reproductive rights to genocide (questions which the figure of the double brings to the forefront). Indeed, what *Battlestar Galactica* and *Fringe* share in common, beyond their repeated focus on the motif of the double—is the way the figure of the doppelganger gets deployed to address contemporary concerns.

9. *Westworld*, the 21st Century Technoculture Take on Doubles

An American science fiction cable television series, *Westworld* debuted on HBO in 2016. The series was created by Jonathan Nolan and Lisa Joy and it is based on a 1973 film of the same name (the film was written and directed by Michael Crichton). Both timely and provocative because of the questions it raises about human rights, agency, and autonomy, the series is set in and around an interactive theme park designed to look like a past representation of the American West. The premise of the series concerns the creation of sentient artificial intelligence (AI), but *Westworld* also revisits the doppelganger motif, specifically through the character of Bernard Lowe, a sentient AI, who is an exact replica of a (now-deceased) human male named Arnold Weber (both Bernard, who is a main character in the television series, and Arnold, who appears in the series via a photograph and multiple flashbacks, are portrayed by actor Jeffrey Wright).

Bernard Lowe, who for a time remains unaware of both the fact that he is an AI and a copy of another person, works as the head of the Delos Corporation's Westworld Programming Division. Since a major revelation of Season 1 is that he, in fact, is not human, the use of the doppelganger figure also works in the series to subvert—and possibly frustrate—viewers' expectations since, thanks in part to the fact that the series moves backward and forward between different timelines, it is not immediately clear that Jeffrey Wright is, in fact, portraying two different characters, one of whom is an AI double. One consequence is that viewers are left questioning their original assumptions while also being pushed to consider how *Westworld* merges ethical and ontological questions through characters such as Bernard Lowe. Another effect this has on the series is that Bernard's own emerging self-awareness informs the plot of the first season—indeed, his journey of self-discovery works as part of *Westworld*'s Season 1 storyline.

Thus, through the character of Bernard Lowe, the television show engages with current debates about ethics and technology while also revisiting age-old concerns about individualism. To be sure, by including the figure of the doppelganger—a concept that is both durable and elastic—the television series brings forth questions about bodies and genre at the same time as the show tests boundaries with respect to both. In this manner, the doppelganger figure functions in the television series as both a cultural vehicle and a means of showcasing current ethical debates about autonomy and human rights. Indeed, *Westworld* (like many of the other texts addressed in this book) calls attention to notions which are being challenged, contested, and redefined in our contemporary era.

Certainly, *Westworld*, like many of the other narratives about doppelgangers discussed in this book, reflects contemporary cultural tensions related to technology and its potentially de-humanizing effects, while also revisiting enduring concerns about identity (recall that the figure of the doppelganger is traditionally associated with the search for the self). The example of doubling depicted in *Westworld* thus also reflects the fact that doppelganger imagery continually "reinvents" itself in response to changing times and shifting cultural anxieties (Totaro).

Created in His Image? Doubling and Representation

Westworld is a television show about an interactive theme park marketed to the ultra-wealthy (the average visit to the park costs $40,000 per day). The futuristic park is designed to look like the American West and is populated by robotic hosts. Visitors to the park are encouraged to live out their fantasies. In fact, in *Westworld*, "every human appetite, no matter how noble or depraved, can be indulged without consequence" ("*Westworld*: The Official Website for the HBO Series").

Although the television show is based on the 1973 film of the same name, there are several notable differences between the film and the HBO series. For one, in the current series, it is virtually impossible to tell the hosts apart from the humans—and this point becomes clear early on in the series. In "Chestnut," the television show's second episode (which originally aired in the U.S. on October 7, 2016), a first-time guest to the park named William (played by Jimmi Simpson) has the following exchange with a host named Angela (played by Talulah Riley):

WILLIAM: Are you real?
ANGELA: Well if you can't tell, does it matter?

Angela's reply here belies the significance of what is at stake since, in *Westworld*'s fictional world, the humans get depicted as being able to behave however they want without repercussion, while the AI hosts are subject to the humans' whims—however violent, strange, or depraved they might be. Indeed, the AI hosts within the theme park are deprived of many of the basic human rights that human beings take for granted, a point which is all the more unsettling when viewers consider how the two are virtually indistinguishable.

In addition to rather self-consciously reflecting the fact that it is difficult to distinguish host from human (a fact hearkened to in the exchange between William and Angela) and thus implicitly critiquing the mistreatment of the AI hosts at the hands of the humans, the television series also, at other points, quite deliberately subverts viewers' expectations with respect to this crucial issue. For example, in the series' pilot, viewers may likely mistake Teddy Flood (played by James Marsden) for a human since he rides into town on a train along with a large group of human guests, but when he is killed only to reappear in the next storyline, it becomes clear that he is actually a host. Teddy's situation also works to foreshadow revelations which come later in the series about hosts who are able to pass as human and the attendant ontological and ethical questions they raise.

Indeed, another major change between the film and HBO series is that, in the 21st century storyline, AI hosts are portrayed as sympathetic figures while many of the human visitors to the park come across as reckless and callous, if not altogether villainous. Christopher Orr explains this different rendering in "Sympathy for the Robot." As he notes in his article, the 1973 movie followed "a decidedly conventional monsters-run-amok plotline" centered on tourists who were visiting an Old West theme park when "robots inevitably glitched, and, led by a mechanized gunslinger played by Yul Brynner, they began massacring the tourists" (Orr). In contrast, HBO's *Westworld* signals a "fundamental shift in moral perspective" (Orr). To be sure, the 2017 series: "Takes this narrative and inverts it by telling the story largely from the perspective of the androids. The series still asks the classic question of what might happen if our creations turned against us, yet it is more interested in the consequences for them than in those for us. The human beings of *Westworld* are, to a considerable degree, supporting players in a drama of android self-actualization" (Orr). As Orr's description suggests, the conceit of the series reflects contemporary concerns about identity and technology—as well as the ethical debates they inevitably raise—subjects which also come to light through the series' depiction of the doppelganger figure.

The television series engages with the doppelganger motif specifically through the character of Arnold Weber and his AI double, Bernard Lowe (note not only that the names "Arnold" and "Bernard" sound similar, but also the fact that Bernard Lowe's name is an anagram for the full name of the human he was modeled after). In the present timeline, Arnold Weber has been dead for decades, yet he nonetheless remains important to the series. At first, his presence works to confuse the audience since it is not immediately clear that Arnold and Bernard are, in fact, two different individuals. When viewers of the series eventually recognize that it has, in fact, been Arnold who has been appearing via flashbacks, they are thus able to glean insights not only about the park's early days, but also about several other of the series' characters—in particular, Dolores Abernathy (played by Evan Rachel Wood) and Dr. Robert Ford (played by Sir Anthony Hopkins).

Together with Dr. Ford, Arnold Weber designed and created the hosts who now populate the park. Dr. Ford reveals to Bernard, who, as the head of the Delos Corporation's Westworld Programming Division, works alongside Ford, that he had a creative partner during the development of the park, and that his partner's name was Arnold. As Dr. Robert Ford explains it, Arnold Weber had much grander plans for the AI hosts: "He wasn't interested in the appearance of intellect or wit. He wanted the real thing. He wanted to create consciousness." When Bernard Lowe makes inquiries about what happened to Arnold, Ford says that Arnold suffered personal tragedy and then withdrew, speaking only with the hosts. Arnold also became consumed by his desire to create consciousness, but before he could bring his vision to fruition, he died. While Arnold Weber's death was officially ruled an accident, revelations come to light in the Season 1 finale which greatly complicate this explanation.

Arnold Weber, in fact, as Joanna Robinson emphasizes, "got very close to waking Dolores up" (Dolores Abernathy is the oldest host in the park), which made him think twice about opening the park to the public. He feared that with the AI hosts so close to achieving consciousness it would be inhumane to subject them to the whims of the human guests. Dr. Robert Ford, however, wanted to move forward with the park's opening, so, in an effort to thwart those plans, Arnold Weber "programmed Dolores to slaughter all her fellow hosts, then kill him" (Robinson). In effect, he "put Dolores into assassin mode. This wasn't an act of free will or consciousness; this was programming" (Robinson). This revelation about Dolores Abernathy's role in Arnold Weber's death is unsettling for viewers, both in terms of what it represents and since it calls into questions assumptions the audience likely may have made about characters and their motivations—it also introduces the notion of the "sleeper agent," a concept which proves important in the series.

To be sure, as Zoe E. Seaman-Grant emphasizes in *Constructing Womanhood and the Female Cyborg: A Feminist Reading of Ex Machina and Westworld*, "Arnold's death hangs over the entire series, with the cause of his death hidden until the final episode of the show" (71). While viewers of the series discover in rapid succession the truth about Bernard Lowe's origins, the details about Arnold Weber's death are withheld until the final moments of the season finale. Viewers learn that Bernard is, in fact, an AI host in Episode 7, "Tromp L'Oeil." Bernard himself gains this insight in Episode 9, "The Well-Tempered Clavier." The revelation about Arnold's death is presented in the latter half of Episode 10 of the series.

These important discoveries come about, in fact, "through two distinct (and distinctly confounding) avenues" (Grubbs). Only by putting together "Bernard's conversations with Ford and Dolores' continued journey to the fringes of *Westworld*," do the puzzle pieces come together (Grubbs). To get the truth out of Dr. Ford, Bernard, "the newly revealed host, cornered his creator and demanded answers about his own origins" (Grubbs). In this manner, the television show reveals that "the soft-spoken programmer was created in the image of Dr. Ford's partner by Ford himself" (Grubbs).

After Arnold Weber's death, Ford created Bernard Lowe in his image. The two are not only physically identical, but they also share mannerisms (including the habit of adjusting their eyeglasses when mulling something over) as well as certain psychological and personality traits. Dr. Ford programmed Bernard to think of himself as a human and, from the point of his creation forward, Bernard worked at Delos Corporation as a member of the staff where he collaborated with Dr. Ford. The other staff members at Delos assumed that he was, in fact, human, yet, the fact that he is AI is part of the reason that Dr. Ford wanted him working alongside him in the first place. In the episode "Trace Decay," the eighth episode of Season 1 (which first aired in the U.S. on November 20, 2016), Dr. Ford confides that he created Bernard because Ford's human staff were not up to the task of programming emotions in the hosts.

The other significant piece of the puzzle, Dolores Abernathy's role in Arnold Weber's death, comes out only after Dolores "begins to have hallucinations of a previous memory in which she kills Arnold after he programs her to kill him" (Seaman-Grant 72). However, the "cause of Dolores's hallucinations is not revealed until the final episode, when we finally learn that Dolores is reliving shooting Arnold over and over again" (Seaman-Grant 72). In the Season 1 finale, Dolores revisits a place she had journeyed to before, on a previous passage of self-discovery. It is not until the penultimate moments of the season that she "found her way back to the town with the white church" and discovered a passageway to a hidden level. She realizes, just as *Westworld*'s viewers do, that in the church, there is "an elevator that took Dolores underground to the secret lab where we've previously seen Bernard interviewing the host. On her way, Dolores passed a door bearing the name that many viewers had been expecting to hear for weeks: Arnold Weber. Now the truth is clear: those interviews were actually memories as well. And it wasn't Bernard who was interviewing Dolores ... it was Arnold himself" (Grubbs). In this manner, *Westworld* wraps up two of the key mysteries that plagued viewers throughout the series' first season.

The Trope of the Sleeper Agent

Revealing that Bernard Lowe was, in fact, created in another's image—and is, hence, an AI doppelganger of the park's co-creator, raises interesting ontological as well as ethical concerns. Indeed, by outing Bernard Lowe as a host, the series also makes it clear his "entire reality—his wife, the dead child he mourns, and his own free will—was constructed by Ford to create the perfect right-hand man" (O'Keefe). Not only is he the perfect partner, but Bernard is also an ideal sleeper agent. Since it was Dr. Ford personally who programmed Bernard as a sleeper agent, he is thus the one responsible for his conflicted identity, a fact which brings with it related questions about Bernard's autonomy and subjectivity. To be sure, with the revelation that "the head of Westworld programming isn't the man we thought he was," the series answers one significant question but raises a host of other concerns (O'Keefe).

Further complicating the issue, Bernard himself remained unaware for much of the first season that he was, in actuality, a host. When he discovers this crucial detail about himself, he also rightly grows suspicious that Dr. Ford may have been keeping other facets of his existence from him, as well. Prompted by the fear that there is much he does not know about himself, he demands that Dr. Ford allow him access to his memories.

When Dr. Ford relents, Bernard learns that he, at Ford's behest, murdered a female colleague, Theresa Cullen (played by Sidse Babett Knudsen). Besides the fact that Bernard sees himself as non-violent, learning that he killed Theresa is particularly unsettling to him since he once had a romantic relationship with her. Viewers learn about their romantic relationship in the last scene of Episode 2, when the two are pictured in bed together. This scene also proves momentous because it provides foreshadowing: Bernard casually mentions to Theresa that the hosts need "practice" talking to seem more human, to which she promptly responds, "Is that what you're doing now? Practicing?"

Bernard has fond memories of the time he spent with Theresa and he is unable to reconcile these with the startling revelation that he, in fact, killed her. Indeed, the thought that he was forced to kill a woman he once had romantic feelings for is too much for him to bear. Unable to make sense of what he did to Theresa, Bernard suffers a breakdown and is unable to form coherent speech. In effect, his personality is destroyed when the submerged persona reappears via his newly reclaimed memories. Perhaps even more disturbing to his psyche, Bernard feels wracked with guilt which he remains unable to process (let alone come to terms with).

As a sleeper agent, "Bernard is not *only* an (unwitting) robot, but also one that will kill when asked. That revelation opens up a world of chilling possibilities and holds the key to some of the larger *Westworld* mysteries" (Robinson). To be sure, not only does this surprising realization cause a crisis for Bernard Lowe, but it also brings with it the question of who might be the mastermind behind *Westworld*'s many other covert happenings. At the same time, the revelation that Bernard has been, all long, a sleeper agent, provokes anxieties related to identity—since, by their very nature, sleeper agents raise questions about what, at essence, is at the root of identity. Moreover, the inclusion of an AI doppelganger who also, it turns out, is a sleeper agent, situates *Westworld* within a larger science fiction tradition.

To be sure, the discovery that Bernard Lowe is actually a sleeper agent demonstrates the series' reliance on a prevalent science fiction trope. Sleeper agents are popular plot devices in fiction (they make frequent appearance in both espionage fiction and science fiction). Fictional representations of sleeper agents reflect—and arguably result from—repeated instances of real-life sleeper agents, individuals who take part in espionage or sedition. Thus, when sleeper agents appear in science fiction texts, they bring to mind not only the ways the figure has appeared within that genre, but also call forth the ways the image has appeared in other modes of storytelling as well as in real life.

The case of Bernard Lowe from *Westworld* is a particularly compelling example since he is an AI as well as a doppelganger *and* unwitting sleeper (indeed, his character raises a number of contemporary questions related to identity and technology), but another noteworthy example of the appearance of sleeper agents in science fiction can be found in *Battlestar Galactica* (a television series which is addressed in the previous chapter of this book) since that show also concerns AI doppelgangers who are sleeper agents—in *BSG*, however, the trope appears due the existence of the many Cylon models. Additionally, the television series *Torchwood* (2006–2011)—in the episodes "Sleeper" and "Adam," in particular—and *The Manchurian Candidate* (2004), a film based on Richard Condon's 1959 novel of the same name, also have plots which center on sleeper agents.

As part of their larger argument, in their book *Different Engines: How Science Drives Fiction and Fiction Drives Science*, Mark Brake and Neil Hook point out how, in science fiction, those who are "indistinguishable from humans" are the perfect sleeper agents and, thus, "well suited for acts of terrorist sabotage" (245). Bernard Lowe functions within *Westworld* in this same capacity, since Ford can control him and therefore use him to carry out espionage and sabotage. Indeed, Bernard Lowe's storyline within the series recalls the popular plot device in fiction of the sleeper agent, who remains inactive until "awakened" (again, this trope appears in *BSG*, *Torchwood*, and other popular science fiction texts).

In a manner quite similar to how the trope traditionally gets deployed, the realization that Bernard is a sleeper agent speaks to the fear of self. His situation reflects the anxiety that surrounds the question of whether it is ever even possible to attain self-knowledge. Moreover, his storyline also confounds traditional explanations about ways to achieve self-knowledge, since the more he learns about himself, the more he questions his character, abilities, and motives—and hence, those qualities which are traditionally understood as being at the very essence of identity.

Indeed, in Bernard Lowe's case, part of the difficulty he faces is trying to reconcile what he has done by killing Theresa Cullen on Dr. Ford's order (he, of course, must also ponder the many other morally questionable actions he has taken at Ford's behest). Bernard's anxiety stems from the fact that his memories exist in direct conflict with his supposed values. Bernard Lowe is, in essence, experiencing what is referred to as a "memory crisis." According to Susan A. George, who discusses the subject in her article "Investigating the Postmodern Memory Crisis on the Small Screen," this "'memory crisis' has become a central theme in the postmodern era" (George 104). As George explains, in the contemporary era, there are real fears associated with "forgetting who we are [and] of losing our way" (115). One way to address this dilemma of self is to "find a memory that 'defines us' as individuals and social beings" (George 115). With respect to Bernard Lowe, his identity is rooted, in part, in his tragic backstory (he lost his young son to a debilitating and, ultimately, terminal illness), but his memories of his personal connection to Theresa Cullen are also what keep him grounded. When confronted with the truth—that he killed his one-time love interest, Theresa Cullen—Bernard suffers a crisis of the sort that Susan A. George describes.

Not only does the uncertainty that Bernard Lowe feels when confronted with the startling reality of his situation communicate much to viewers about his conflicted emotions as a character, but it also reveals a larger cultural ambivalence about identity in the postmodern world. As Paul Grainge points out in his book *Monochrome Memories: Nostalgia and Style in Retro America* (2002), during the postmodern era, there exist widespread cultural anxieties surrounding the "instability and unreliability" of memory (5). While Grainge acknowledges that "the desire for memory as stable, reassuring, and constant has always been plagued by the fear of its instability and unreliability," these fears have become compounded in contemporary times (5). Indeed, the transformative possibilities of postmodernism have made the "issues of memory crisis seem even more intractable" (Grainge 5). Bernard's situation in the first season of *Westworld* thus reflects these anxieties of the current era.

To be sure, both viewers of *Westworld* and the character Bernard himself are accordingly forced to consider whether, in his case, there is any true "self" beneath the surface. Again, this anxiety which *Westworld* both produces and reflects has to do with the fear of the "decentering" of self. Questions surrounding the television series' representation of Bernard Lowe, not only as an AI, but also as a doppelganger and sleeper agent, raise ancillary concerns related to identity formation, as well. What, at its essence, is identity? Is identity merely a performance or an iterative act, or is there reason to suggest there is something more?

During the eighth episode of *Westworld*, Dr. Ford addresses these issues as part of a larger discussion where he reveals his stance on the nature of human consciousness. According to Dr. Ford, "there is no threshold that makes us greater than the sum of our parts, no inflection point at which we become fully alive. We can't define consciousness because consciousness does not exist." What human beings mistakenly interpret as consciousness, according to Ford, is no different than the state of mind the artificial hosts in the theme park experience. Thus, he suggests that consciousness may, in fact, be little more than an illusion. As Kwame Opam puts it, *Westworld* brings to the screen a "simulated Wild West peopled with robots that may or may not have consciousness." This question, which is at the heart of the television series, pushes viewers to consider the nature of consciousness (not only within the series, but also more broadly)—and it thus provokes anxieties for a 21st century audience, since identity is being contested and redefined in contemporary times.

Bodily Anxieties in/and *Westworld*

Beyond provoking anxieties about the nature of self and the existence of consciousness, the series also pushes boundaries with its representations of bodies—and thus, *Westworld* also brings bodily anxieties to the forefront. As Kaye Mitchell argues in her article "Bodies That Matter: Science Fiction, Technoculture, and the Gendered Body," the genre of "SF allows for the production of radical (gendered and un-gendered, hybrid, cyborgian) bodies that impel us to reflect upon our own understanding of 'the body' and upon the ways in which bodies are viewed and regulated in the social world." This is particularly the case with "the discourse surrounding cyborgs" since the "boundaries of the body itself and, relatedly, the boundaries of the 'human' are at stake" (Mitchell). Indeed, as Mitchell emphasizes, the suggestion of "much technocultural theory is that contemporary technology has rendered these boundaries unstable, permeable, negotiable." Using the lens of technocultural theory, it is possible to see how the HBO series *Westworld* calls into question these contemporary concerns, which have emerged as our relationship with technology has changed.

To be sure, *Westworld* highlights the degree to which human beings have been co-evolving, and continue to co-evolve, with our technology. In this respect, the series calls to mind—and makes manifest—situations such as those described by scholars and cultural historians like Donna Haraway, N. Katherine Hayles, Bruno Latour, Elaine Graham, and Timothy Taylor, all of whom—in their various ways—emphasize how the rapid emergence of new technologies in recent decades has worked to accentuate the view that contemporary life is defined by our relationship with our tools and machines. In this manner, bodies therefore become the sites of ideological conflict and thus also become contested spaces where cultural anxieties become manifest.

Anxieties thus result from the fact that, as humans, we are becoming ever more reliant on technology. Consequently, as Amanda Fernbach argues in her book *Fantasies of Fetishism: From Decadence to the Post Human*, there exists a cultural preoccupation about the body in the age of technology, one which emerges in science fiction texts through depictions of the "hybrid technologized body" (3). While debates related to the merging of human and machine have historically—and all too frequently—centered on female bodies, it is worth noting that, in *Westworld*, controversies also come to light due to the presence of male characters who are hosts, such as Teddy Flood, Hector Escaton (played by Rodrigo Santoro), and, in particular, Bernard Lowe (an AI doppelganger, who is also a sleeper agent).

Indeed, as a series, *Westworld* raises important ethical and ontological questions that are brought to the forefront through the presence of male bodies. Bernard Lowe works especially well as a case-in-point to demonstrate that *Westworld*—and, by extension, the genre of science fiction—is concerned with representations that go beyond the "female only fem-bots" stereotype. Jeffery Wright's performances as both Bernard Lowe and Arnold Weber put him in the position of portraying both a creator and a creation, so this acting role presents him with the opportunity to occupy the subject position (when he portrays Arnold Weber, a brilliant scientist who is the park's co-creator) while also giving voice to the experiences of a being who has been subordinated (when he plays the role of Bernard Lowe, an unwitting sleeper agent whom Dr. Ford exerts control over).

To be sure, because he can so convincingly play both roles (the role of the park's co-creator with a conscience *and* the role of an AI host), Jeffery Wright's performance in the television series underscores the uncanny similarities between human and host, a conceit which remains important not only to his depiction of these characters, but which also proves to be a central concern of the series. In the case of the characters Arnold Weber and Bernard Lowe, their identical appearance makes it impossible to tell them apart—and thus, prevents viewers from really knowing who is beneath the surface. In this manner, Wright's portrayal helps to blur the line between natural and artificial life forms and thus forces the show's audience to reconsider their concept of what it means to be human.

Moreover, in the case of his portrayal of Bernard Lowe and Arnold

Weber, because actor Jeffrey Wright is an African American male co-starring in a popular science fiction series, the series complicates—at the same time as it subverts stereotypes about—race and ethnicity (and how they are traditionally depicted on television). This feature is particularly noteworthy considering that *Westworld* is a science fiction text, a genre known for both appealing to white males and for playing to the white male gaze. In this manner, the series pushes boundaries at the same time as it raises questions about contemporary depictions of racialized and othered bodies on screen.

Westworld as Social Commentary

Alongside provoking cultural anxieties related to bodies, the series also raises ethical questions about the treatment of the AI hosts. In this manner, the series functions as social commentary by calling attention to humans' violent nature. In the series, human visitors have the freedom to indulge in an almost limitless range of activities, but this freedom, as Ellen R. Menger points out in *Casual and Hardcore Players in HBO's Westworld*, "seems to be expressed mainly in the form of many instances of violence being inflicted by the park's visitors upon the robot hosts" (1). Moreover, due to "the highly realistic humanoid design of the robot hosts, visitors' acts of violence towards them evoke questions about visitors' morals," especially in scenes where the human guests are "shown to wantonly harm, abuse, and even kill the park's hosts simply for fun and a thrill" (Menger 1). Indeed, as series, *Westworld* takes care to show "how visitors choose to engage in violent and immoral behavior in a setting that does not necessarily" invite it (Menger 1).

The series' many depictions of humans as violent works as a point of contrast between humans and the AI hosts and also demonstrates a shift from the 1973 film. As Emily Nussbaum explains in her article "The Meta-Politics of *Westworld*," in the HBO series, they have "transformed the black hat from a cyborg into a human, who approaches the theme park as if it were a video game. And, crucially, they've shifted the story's sympathies from the visitors to the cyborgs, known within *Westworld* as 'hosts.'" According to Nussbaum's reading of the series, not only are the hosts sympathetic, but they are "far more layered than the tourists who exploit them and the technicians who service them." The fact that a theme park exists where "hosts are raped, shot, and tortured" only to, at night, go to bed and "forget everything, to start all over again" shows the startling difference between humans and hosts, but it also does much to paint humanity in a negative light (while offering a much more sympathetic portrait of the victimized AI).

The result is that the series presents as "a multivalent metaphor," a play "on the 'brain wipes' that appear in a lot of science fiction, like *Eternal Sunshine of the Spotless Mind*" (Nussbaum). The series also brings to mind political narratives about "vulnerable citizens forced to repress atrocities so that their nation can drape a patriotic story over its ugly history" (Nussbaum). Not only a series about the creation of artificial consciousness, *Westworld* is also a television show about what it means to be human and, indeed, by portraying humans in a negative light, the series functions as a critique of the darker aspects of human nature.

Certainly, the case of Bernard Lowe, an AI doppelganger, works as part of this broader critique. Created in the image of the park's human co-founder, he is so very human-like, yet he is not human. Instead he occupies a liminal space from which he can call attention to humanity's flaws. Thus, the violence he enacts (which, significantly, is at the behest of Dr. Robert Ford) reflects the violent nature of humans who, if Dr. Ford is any kind of example, will behave however they want without regard to how their actions affect others, whether human or AI.

Indeed, as a being whom Dr. Ford not only has created but one whom he maintains control over—to the point that he forces him to carry out his dirty work—Bernard Lowe functions as a compelling example of the way humans will exploit others for their gain. Dr. Ford's willingness to exploit Bernard comes across as all the more sinister when viewers recall that, in creating Bernard, he gave him an elaborate tragic backstory. Although Ford claims that this was necessary to form the cornerstone of Bernard's personality, audiences of the series must wonder if he made Bernard suffer needlessly.

Bernard Lowe's (Double) Role in the Series

Yet, Bernard Lowe does much more in the series than call attention to the fact that *Westworld* offers a degree of social critique through its storylines. As a being who remains, for so long, unaware of both the fact that he is an AI and a copy of another person, Bernard highlights the instability of identity in the 21st century—and, he thus reflects the fear of self, a timeless concerns which persists even into contemporary times. As a character, Bernard also forces viewers of the series to reconsider their original assumptions about him since *Westworld* initially withholds and then, only later, slowly divulges information about his nature and origins. By making its audience second-guess themselves, the television series provokes anxieties about the fear of the other, as well. Anxieties about the self and other have long been reflected in storylines about doubles and, as the example of *Westworld* suggests, these concerns remain both troubling and relevant to this day.

10. Clones and Cultural Anxieties in *Orphan Black*

The Canadian science fiction television series *Orphan Black*, which debuted in the U.S. on BBC America in March 2013, stars Tatiana Maslany playing the role of Sarah Manning and several of her fellow clones, all born by in vitro fertilization. Through the various characters Maslany plays, as well as through many of the episodes' plot-lines, the series revisits the age-old debate of nature versus nurture while also raising provocative and timely questions about agency, identity, and human rights in the 21st century. A show with many of the hallmarks of both quality and cult TV, *Orphan Black* is a television program which addresses on a fundamental level what it means be human. As part of this project, the television show offers a lens for fans of the series to view urgent current debates and, for this reason, *Orphan Black* proves to be an important cultural product.

Yet, as a popular television series, *Orphan Black* also highlights and reflects our cultural preoccupations with identity and individualism, both of which are being challenged at the same time as new spaces and technologies are made available through which we can explore and express ourselves. Indeed, *Orphan Black* demonstrates a sustained engagement with 21st century controversies as well as a continued focus on multiplicity, a concept which has gained new significance in the 21st century due to developments in reproductive and cyber technologies.

The Intersection of Cult and Quality Television

Orphan Black occupies a unique position among contemporary television programs: the show exists at the intersection of quality and cult

TV. According to Robert J. Thompson, who defines the characteristics of "quality television" in his book *Television's Second Golden Age*, the denotation quality television gets reserved for programming that breaks rules by defying standard parameters and creating new narrative territory. A hallmark of quality television is that critics praise it for being "unlike anything they've ever seen on television." Indeed, according to Thompson's definition, quality TV provokes the boundaries in terms of both its content and genre: the subject matter tends toward the controversial and quality television resists easy generic classification by mixing older genres together.

Orphan Black, frequently hailed by critics as "groundbreaking," exists as a shining example of quality television. Not only has its star, Tatiana Maslany, succeeded at the unprecedented task of playing a dozen (and counting) different characters within the same show, but the production of the series involves intricate filming, particularly in the frequent scenes featuring Maslany playing multiple parts (for these scenes, the production team films the scene numerous times using motion control cameras mounted on dollies to replicate the movement between each shot). The show's emphasis on technique highlights the production team's commitment to quality, and *Orphan Black's* sophisticated visual style marks it as quality, as well.

As Jonathan Bignell argues in "Seeing and Knowing: Reflexivity and Quality," design aspects work to set quality television apart: "*mise-en-scene* and the foregrounding of visual style are not only markers of quality in terms of production value, but also perform seeing and knowing as meaning-making activities carried out for and in television" (Bignell 166). Not only does the series push the limits in terms of technique, but Orphan Black also provokes boundaries in terms of its thematic concerns by addressing a range of prescient and timely controversies including human cloning, stem cell research, reproductive technologies, and the patenting of DNA. The show also includes a transgender character, Tony (also played by Maslany), thus, again pushing boundaries in its representation. Referring to the existence of Tony, J.M. Suarez describes *Orphan Black* as groundbreaking because of "the almost casual way in which sexuality and gender is presented."

Though *Orphan Black* fits the definition of quality TV, the show has such a large cult following that many critics have also categorized it as cult television. For example, writing for the *Hollywood Reporter*, Tim Goodman praised Maslany for helping to "rocket BBC America's *Orphan Black* to cult status as one of television's most compelling genre series," and Ed Stockly, writing for the *LA Times*, describes *Orphan Black* as a "cult science fiction thriller." Fans of the series have started a rather large and active Facebook group called "Clone Club," which describes itself as a "big family"; the group invites discussions and sees itself as a place to share thoughts about the series. As evidenced by this Facebook group and the large amount chatter on this and other forms of social media about the series, *Orphan Black* seems to have tapped into cult fandom.

Far from being incidental, the role played by fans of *Orphan Black* does much to mark the show as cult television. As Matt Hills persuasively argues in his book *Fan Culture*, in our digital age—and thanks, in part, to social media sites—fans today are different from their predecessors. Indeed, as Hills emphasizes, there is an emerging discourse of cult fandom that can be harnessed in new ways in the 21st century because of social media and the internet (xi). Taking this point even further, Mark Jancovich and James Lyons, who also discuss the relationship between cult TV and fandom in their anthology *Cult TV, the Industry and Fans*, describe a new category of cult television that came about in the late 20th and early 21st centuries. The reasons behind the rise of this new category remain complex (changing industry norms, actors' relationships with fans, and various other factors all contribute its emergence), but, as Jancovich and Lyons highlight, recent iterations of cult fandom prove to be markedly different in recent decades.

As a popular science fiction series that transcends genre, *Orphan Black* has tapped into this new form of cult fandom at the same time as the show also has proved to be quality television. Existing at the intersection of cult and quality television, *Orphan Black* presents a timely and prescient exploration of concerns such as agency, autonomy, and human rights. By responding to a cultural moment through its engagement with 21st century practices (such as cloning, IVF, and the patenting of DNA) and through its inclusion of controversial characters (such as the transgender character, Tony), the series appeals to viewers who are interested in seeing contemporary debates play out on screen. At the same time, however, the series also addresses our collective anxiety about becoming multiple as a consequence of the new spaces and technologies now available through which we can explore and express ourselves.

Multiplicity and Cultural Anxieties

The initial mystery that begins the series gets introduced when Sarah Manning (Maslany) sees her doppelganger, Elizabeth "Beth" Childs (also played by Maslany), commit suicide at a train station. From this point forward, the plot of *Orphan Black* gets propelled by a series of questions relating to cloning and Manning's realization that she is one of many clones, so, from its inception, *Orphan Black* has been—and remains—a television show about multiplicity. Though the series proves engaging because of quality acting, engaging storylines, good writing, and impressive cinematic technique, the television show has also, importantly, tapped in to a cultural moment: in *Orphan Black*, we see both the promise and potential dangers of multiplicity. This aspect of *Orphan Black* is in keeping with a recent trend; indeed, storylines that center on twins, doppelgangers, or (as in the case of *Orphan Black*) clones have gained popularity in recent years and many 21st century television programs feature doubles (whether they be twins, clones, doppelgangers, or some other form). What this series has succeeded in doing is to not only raise provocative questions about individuality and agency, but to push the boundaries about what these issues mean to a 21st century audience.

To be sure, society's fascination with—as well as anxiety about—multiplicity has its roots in numerous medical, scientific, and technological developments that have made possible in the 21st century things which just decades ago were the stuff of science fiction. Though many believe we are still years away from successfully cloning humans, the cloning of animals has been practiced regularly since 1996 when Dolly, the infamous sheep, was born (she was cloned by Dr. Ian Wilmut and his team at the Roslin Institute near Edinburgh). Among humans, fertility treatments are now quite common; not only have they become affordable in recent years, but the practice has also become more normalized.

One result of this is that we have seen a real spike in the number of twins (and other multiples) born. Indeed, thanks to what has been dubbed the "IVF Effect," there really *are* more twins nowadays, a phenomenon that has been widely reported (recall Alexis C. Madrigal's April 2014 *Atlantic Monthly* article, where she notes that there are about a million so-called "extra" twins that have been born). Due to a handful of factors, chief among them being an increase in infertility treatments, specifically *in vitro* fertilization and ovulation stimulation medications, women are having twins at a higher rate than has ever been seen before.

In *Orphan Black*, there are actually both twins and clones featured— Sarah and her sister Helena are identical twins born from the same mother and, in fact, they are mirror images of each other (Helena's heart is on the right side of her body), and there are also an unspecified number of characters who are clones. While twins are becoming more commonplace in our society, clones are still a thing of, if not science fiction, at least fringe science. In this sense, *Orphan Black* both relies upon the long-popular trope of television twins while also pushing the boundaries through the inclusion of the many characters who are clones. Through these characters and the dilemmas they face, *Orphan Black* features an extended meditation on identity. Not only do we see, time and again, these characters asserting their agency, individuality, and human rights, but the television series pushes us to consider evolving legal and ontological concerns: If you can patent a gene, what's to stop scientists or corporations from patenting a whole person (which is what happens in *Orphan Black*)? What would it mean to be human in a post-human world?

After Sarah witnesses Beth's suicide, she slowly unravels the mystery surrounding her and her sister clones' origins. Over the course of Seasons 1 through 3, Sarah discovers that she was created as part of a scientific experiment code-named Project Leda, wherein there were created an unspecified number of clones, the majority of whom were born in 1984 to various women by in vitro fertilization (in Season 2, we discover that there is actually one surviving clone who is much younger that the rest. Named Charlotte, she, unlike the others, wasn't born in 1984; in fact, she is still a child). As more information gets revealed about Project Leda and the individual clones, we learn that the clones share certain personality traits, for, as Cosima (one of the clones) notes, they all have a tendency to be impulsive and make rash decisions, but beyond a few core traits, the clones vary greatly and, cumulatively, they represent a wide spectrum of experience. Environment seems to play a role in the clones' divergent experiences and lifestyle choices, but the show also allows other potential explanations for why their personalities differ.

Sarah Manning, the first clone we are introduced to, and the one the series follows most closely, is a small-time grifter. She was raised in a foster family and struggles to raise her own daughter, Kira. Sarah (to date) is the only one who has so far been "successful" in her fertility (though at the end of Season 3, it is revealed that Helena, Sarah's twin, is pregnant, and her pregnancy continues to be a point of focus in Seasons 4 and 5). Indeed, in Season 2, Ethan Duncan (a scientist involved in the cloning project and a man who raised Rachel Duncan, another of the clones) tells Rachel that the clones were all "barren by design." Beth Childs, the second clone we learn about, is now deceased, but she worked as a police detective. Alison Hendrix is a suburban Toronto housewife who is involved in community theatre and married to Donnie; with him, she is raising two (adopted) children. Sarah labels Alison a "soccer mom," but Alison's suburban life is far from idyllic. She struggles with substance abuse, cheats on her husband with her neighbor Aynsley's husband, she helps her husband cover-up a crime he committed (Donnie shoots and kills Dr. Leekie, a scientist working for DYAD, and Alison helps him hide the body), and she has a role in her neighbor's Aynsley's death.

Helena, who is introduced as a serial killer (she is, at one point, hunting down and killing other clones, her sisters), presents as quite formidable, but she becomes a sympathetic figure, as well. Both victim and avenger, Helena eventually forms a strong bond with Sarah (her twin sister and "mirror image") and she starts to work with her other "sisters," as well. Helena, however, is not only a hunter, but she is being hunted at various points throughout the series—and by several different factions, it seems. For example, the end of Season 2 ends with her captured and in a precarious position which she spends the first part of Season 3 trying (ultimately successfully) to escape. Even in Season 5, a now very pregnant Helena continues to be relentlessly pursued (though by a different faction at this point). Cosima Niehaus, another clone, is a scientist who studies genetics. When audiences are first introduced to Cosima, she is a Ph.D. student studying microbiology at the University of Minnesota, but she eventually starts working at DYAD institute. Rachel Duncan (who was raised by Ethan and his wife) is financially well-off, but ruthless (going as far as ordering the extermination of several of her sister clones) and barren, a fact which upsets her greatly. She works as high-ranking executive within the Dyad Institute. Beyond these women, the core group of clones, which remain the focus of *Orphan Black*, there are several other known clones, both alive and deceased (these include Katja, M.K., Krystal, Danielle, and Jennifer, to name just a few of the Leda clones) and the series suggests that more still could be discovered as new episodes are released.

The Project Leda Clones and Their Different Paths

As the clones described above demonstrate, though these women are genetically identical, they have taken very different paths in their lives— and the range of their experiences is something the clones themselves remain acutely aware of. For example, in Season 2 Helena acknowledges the diverse paths she and her sister clones have taken when she weaves a narrative that combines elements of her past with details some from her sisters' life experiences. During "To Hound Nature in Her Wanderings"

(Episode 6 of the second season of *Orphan Black*, which first aired in the U.S. on May 24, 2014), Helena visits a bar, having momentarily eluded one group of would-be-captors (religious extremists called the "Proletheans"), and she meets a young man named Jesse. She likes Jesse, so during the evening they talk, drink, arm wrestle, dance, and kiss (Helena goes as far as to call him her "boyfriend"). During their evening conversation, Helena tells Jesse the following:

> HELENA: In Ukraine, I was police detective. I shot many criminals.
> JESSE: Ukraine, huh? I've never been further than Sioux Falls, myself.
> HELENA: Then, I was brilliant scientist, but I quit to be with my family.
> JESSE: Oh, come on. Don't tell me you're spoken for.
> HELENA: Divorced. After rehab drinking problems. But now, I am with my sestra, having adventures.

Most of the details she reveals to Jesse in this exchange aren't actually about her own life; rather, they are about her sisters' lives. The part about living in the Ukraine is an actual detail from her life (as is her comment about "having adventures" with her "sestra"), but the other details correspond to other Project Leda clones: Beth was the detective; Cosima is the brilliant scientist; and, the reference about quitting a career to be with family is a nod to Alison, as is the mention of spending time in "rehab." So, though while much of what Helena tells Jesse is an elaborate fiction, it is a fiction made up of details from her sister-clones' lives. Her narrative here is worth exploring for she reveals the interconnectedness between the clones. She also speaks of a wide range of possibilities in terms of women's experiences, and she points to how different environments and life choices can shape one's path. In sum, this conversation highlights the promise and potential of multiplicity, which is one of the show's themes.

A similar occurrence takes place in Season 5, when Alison tries to reconcile her role in relation to the other Project Leda clones. In the episode "Beneath Her Heart" (Episode 3 of the fifth and final season of *Orphan Black*, which first aired in the U.S. on June 24, 2017), Alison, in fact, struggles, in both the present timeline and via a series of flashbacks (where viewers see her first confronting the fact that she is a clone), with identity-related questions. The flashbacks are particularly revealing since they display how first learning she was a clone pushed her to both question her life choices and examine her concept of self-hood (indeed, Alison's sense of identity was thrust headlong into a tailspin, thanks to this revelation!). During one of these flashbacks, Alison looks into a mirror and contemplates both her identity and the choices she has made. "Why do I have this face? I could have been born with many faces—I could have been a cop or a scientist, but I wound up microwaving mini pizzas and chauffeuring kids to circus camp. Why this life?"

Alison is, of course, alluding to the paths that two of the other Project Leda clones went down—the cop is a direct reference to Beth, and the scientist she speaks of is Cosima. Alison is being forced to re-examine her life choices in the face of learning how dissimilar her sister clones' experiences have been from her own. While this line of questioning reveals much about Alison's own internal psychological struggles, it also speaks to the series' over-arching concern: the changing nature of identity in a postmodern world. Moreover, this scene works to emphasize how contemporary representations of multiplicity provoke cultural anxieties.

Why *does* multiplicity resonate with a 21st century audience? While contemporary life provides numerous opportunities to reinvent ourselves, to adapt to these roles and rapidly advancing technologies, we need to be able to play different parts. Human engagement with technology promises new freedoms and potentials, yet but also brings with it new problems. The same tools we use have the ability to change us—for better or worse. Indeed, it is also true that technology fundamentally alters us and how we see ourselves.

While many view this change as positive and one full of potential, it can also serve as a source of anxiety for others—especially since the effects are so pervasive. For all of its promise, multiplicity can also function as a source of tension because, despite the many benefits that it may promise, "multiplicity is not viable if it means shifting among personalities that cannot communicate," a point that Turkle emphasizes. Indeed, as she makes clear, "multiplicity is not acceptable if it means being confused to a point of immobility" (Turkle 258).

These are some of the many concerns that the television show *Orphan Black* addresses. Through its characters—primarily the Project Leda clones—and plot, the timely television series underscores how questions related to identity have become even more complicated in recent years (largely because of contemporary technological advances). The power that computers and other forms of technology affords us to be multiple also opens up new spaces for us—indeed, there is plenty of room for promise as well as new anxieties, particularly those related to identity and autonomy. *Orphan Black* responds to these anxieties while also pushing audiences to consider what it means to be human in the early 21st century.

Indeed, a primary way the show engages with these questions is through the clones themselves. Sarah and her sister-clones remain acutely invested in demonstrating their autonomy, identity, and individuality. These concerns resonate throughout the series, with many episodes of *Orphan Black* reflecting this theme. Just as Teresa Jusino emphasizes in her recent discussion of the series, "*Orphan Black* is, in large part, about women fighting for their bodily autonomy." To be sure, viewers of the series see the Project Leda clones struggling, but also speaking out against those who would seek to use, abuse, or label them.

Their resistance to those who seek to control them is so important to the series that even the promotional trailers and stills released call attention to it. For example, prior to the beginning of Season 3, promos highlighted the way that the Project Leda clones were taking an especially strong and active stance against any such efforts to control them by using stills which feature Tatiana Maslany, as several of the clones, alternately asserting: "I am not your toy" (Alison); "I am not your weapon" (Helena); "I am not your experiment" (Cosima); and "I am not your property" (Sarah). Through these proclamations, Alison, Helena, Cosima, and Sarah exhibit their individuality at the same time as they assert their agency by demanding their fundamental human rights.

It is worth noting that, paradoxically, through these statements (from the promotional stills), the Project Leda clones are simultaneously refusing to be labeled by DYAD or any others who want to lay claim to them, while also highlighting how others have typically perceived them. Alison, who feels like she has been both toyed with and played with, refuses to play along any longer. Helena, who has been weaponized by religious fundamentalists and then, later, captured by a paramilitary group (she escapes their custody before we fully comprehend what they had intended to do with her), refuses to be used any longer. Cosima, a scientist herself who has now fallen ill, refuses to be further experimented on.

In the case of Cosima, she is also responding to her past treatment by Dr. Leekie. Going back to Season 2, Cosima once had a conversation with Dr. Leekie where he revealed that he saw her as a subject worth examining. Leekie tells her, "You could be on the cover of *Scientific American*." Cosima, however, reminds him that they don't put scientists on the cover, to which Leekie pointedly replies, "Well, every rule needs to be broken." Leekie's remarks suggest that he sees Cosima as more of a scientific experiment than a scientist. To him, she is the scientific breakthrough, rather than being the scientist who makes a breakthrough.

In the case of Sarah, DYAD sees her as their property. They want to lay claim to her body and her daughter Kyra (she is unique among the clones since she has had a healthy pregnancy resulting in a healthy child).

In fact, during Season 2, Rachel has gone as far as to attempt to steal one of Sarah's ovaries by forcing her to undergo an involuntary, and medically unnecessary, oophorectomy, but Sarah escapes.

Although different individuals and diverse forces—sometimes ones with competing or contradictory ideologies—have attempted to control Alison, Helena, Cosima, Sarah, and the other Project Leda clones, they share in common a desire to strip these women of their autonomy in favor of using them for their own designs. Yet, by speaking up for themselves and banding together, the Project Leda clones assert not only their agency and identity, but they also demand human rights and to be seen as fully and functionally human, despite their origins. In this way, the television series makes a bold statement about what it means to be human in our increasingly post-human world.

Through the various scenarios the clones of *Orphan Black* encounter, the television show offers a lens for fans of the series to consider current debates related to politics, women's bodies, religious extremism, and gender identity (to name just a few of the series' concerns) and, for this reason, *Orphan Black* proves to be an important cultural product. Yet, as a popular television series which exists at the intersection of quality and cult TV, *Orphan Black* also shines a light on our cultural preoccupations with autonomy, personal freedoms, and individualism, all of which are being challenged at the same time as new spaces and technologies are made available through which we can discover and express ourselves.

11. Cinematic Clones in *The Island* and *Oblivion*

Orphan Black, with its engagement with current debates related to politics, women's bodies, religious extremism, and gender identity, stands out as an important cultural product that relies upon representations of doubling—in particular through the presence of the Project Leda clones—to examine contemporary cultural anxieties. This noteworthy television series, however, is not the only example of a clone narrative brought to life on the screen. Indeed, contemporary cinema is rife with examples of storylines that feature clones—and, in many cases, these films use the figure to bring up timely questions about the relationship between identity, memory, and technology.

Two such examples can be found in the big-budget films *The Island* (2005), directed by Michael Bay, and *Oblivion* (2013), directed by Joseph Kosinski (and based on his graphic novel of the same name). *The Island* follows Lincoln Six Echo (played by Ewan McGregor) and Jordan Two Delta (played by Scarlett Johannsson), apparent survivors of an environmental catastrophe who live in an underground bunker. They, just like the other supposed survivors, are waiting to win a "lottery" which they believe will send them to an island paradise far away, but Lincoln Six Echo accidentally discovers the bleak reality of their existence: they are actually clones, created to provide replacement organs for the originals they were copied from. *Oblivion* centers on Jack Harper (played by Tom Cruise), a tech repairman who lives in close orbit to a devastated, radioactive Earth. While Jack has been led to believe that he is one of a small group of human survivors and that he will soon join the others on Titan (the site of a human colony), he, like the protagonists of *The Island*, also soon learns that the story he has been fed is an elaborate fiction. The truth is that he is actually one of many clones who have been created by hostile aliens who need help with clean-up on Earth.

Beyond the fact that both films boast A-list stars and cutting-edge special effects, *The Island* and *Oblivion* share in common the fact that they are clone narratives. Moreover, both films feature individuals who are, at first, unaware of their nature (meaning the fact that they are clones), and then, only later, come to realize that they have been created for dubious purposes. In both cases, the process of clones coming to terms with the reality of their existence works to forward the action and, eventually, bring about resolution to their respective plots. Like so many other storylines that involve clones, both movies question the ethics of human cloning while also provoking cultural anxieties of the current era.

Ethics, Autonomy and the Commodification of Clones in *The Island*

Set in the near future, *The Island* envisions a society where cloning technology has progressed to the point that it is possible to create genetically identical copies of humans for those who want an "insurance policy." As Kate O'Riordan describes it in her article "Human Cloning in Film: Horror, Ambivalence, Hope," the film's audience is invited to imagine human cloning technologies operating in "the service of commodified health care" (153). In this scenario, "the production of full body clones, DNA matched to original donors, has been 'perfected'" and, thus the film "represents human reproductive cloning as a health care technology" (O'Riordan 153).

The intricate process of creating clones (a procedure which also gets described to prospective clients at one point in the film) can be witnessed in a scene which shows fully formed adult clones maturing, only to later emerge from artificial wombs. Affluent clients, such as entrepreneurs, professional athletes, and celebrities, have paid handsomely to have exact copies of themselves made in case they need a perfectly matched organ or tissue donor. While these clients have a rudimentary understanding of the process, they have been led to believe that their clones will exist in a "permanent vegetative state" until such time as they are needed for their organs. Those who work in the facility know very well that this is a lie that has been fed to their potential clients; however, even though they interact with the clones (and see on a daily basis how human-like they are), they nonetheless have convinced themselves that the clones are subhuman.

Dr. Bernard Merrick (played by Sean Bean), the key scientist in charge of the project, exemplifies this mentality. He reveals his feelings about the clones quite clearly in a scene where he also boasts about his role in their creation: "I have discovered the Holy Grail of science. I give life. The agnates, they're simply tools, instruments. They have no souls." Merrick, it seems, is so blinded by his scientific ambition that he fails to consider that the clones are anything other than mere "tools."

While the clones are sentient, they nonetheless remain—for a time, at least—unaware of the fact that they are, in actuality, clones. Indeed, the biotechnology corporation which has created them quite deliberately keeps them in the dark about their nature. The scientists there have come up with an elaborate story that the Earth's surface is uninhabitable and they have further convinced the clones that they are human survivors of a recent catastrophe. This grim fiction is the means by which they convince the clones to go along with the rigid structure of life in the compound, going as far as to have the clones submit to invasive tests designed to monitor their health.

By feeding the clones this story, the scientists have managed to hide the truth, which is that the clones have been created to provide replacement parts for their human counterparts. According to John Horn, who discusses *The Island* in an *LA Times* film review, the "core conceit" of the film concerns "a shadowy corporate enterprise cloning the rich so as to supply them with back-up organs and tissue or 'insurance policies'" (E5). While most of the clones featured in *The Island* exist so that the can serve as organ donors for their originals (should the need arise), the film also represents the practice of using clones for reproductive purposes—this practice comes to light through a scene which reveals that a female clone has been used as a surrogate mother. Both practices are ethically problematic because they de-humanize, at the same time as they deny agency to, one group of individuals (the clones) in the service of another (their originals).

Though the film paints the corporation behind the cloning technology as unscrupulous, *The Island* nonetheless treats the practice of cloning as normalized. In fact, sales pitches for the types of services the biotechnology provider offers appear rather conspicuously in the film. As O'Riordan points out, "the image of cloning as an elite and desirable health care option is emphasized in a scene in *The Island* in which the fictional biotechnology company pitches the cloning service to prospective clients. The wealth and celebrity status of the clients is emphasized" (153).

As scenes such as the one O'Riordan alludes to suggest, the film overtly raises questions about the ethical limits of biomedical advancement by considering whether (and to what degree) science should operate independently of ethical concerns. At the same time, the film's plot highlights the increasing commodification of medical services, thus both indicting current practices and serving as a cautionary tale about the ethical consequences of cloning. In this manner, the film works to "overtly criticize the dehumanizing power of commodity science" (O'Riordan 154–155). In this respect, the film also considers the relationship between capitalism and bioethics.

All of these debates invariably bring with them questions about whether medical and scientific advancement should progress without first considering corresponding ethical implications. In other words, should science be governed by what we *can* do or what we *should* do? As bioethicist Art Caplan (who serves as the director of the Center for Bioethics at the University of Pennsylvania) notes, in the current century, "technology is moving in biomedicine at an incredibly fast pace on many different fronts" (Dahlstrom). Caplan discusses ethical conundrums and the boundaries between what science can do and what it should do in his book *Smart Mice, Not-So-Smart People*; as he explains it, he believes that there has already been "ethical fallout from progress in the life sciences" (Dahlstrom). He adds that "it is very clear that the 21st century will be the age of the life sciences where new knowledge of our genes, brains, and physiology will confront us with incredible choices and challenges" (Dahlstrom). Concerns similar to those that Caplan sees as emerging in the coming years get reflected in *The Island*, a film which brings these debates to the big screen.

As part of its discussion about the ethics of cloning, *The Island* positions human against clone, a maneuver that, in fact, ends up calling into question the humanity of both groups. In the case of the human scientists represented, their overwhelmingly callous disregard for ethical concerns in creating clones (as well as their failure to consider the rights of clones) makes them appear monstrous. With respect to the situation the clones find themselves in, their status—legal, moral, and ontological—remains very much up for debate.

To be sure, as Graham emphasizes, as "new reproductive technologies, cloning, and genetic modification" emerge, these advancements "promise to engender a future in which the boundaries between humanity, technology, and nature will be ever more malleable" (3). Simply put, as medical technology advances, the line between human and other will get further blurred, if not altogether dissolved, a fact that also makes it difficult to locate the differences between categories of beings, such as humans and clones. This difficulty in distinguishing human from other is symptomatic of the identity crisis taking place in our contemporary era and it also reflects our fragmented, postmodern state of identity. As Steve Jones argues in his article "Cyber-Punk: Cyberpunk and Information Technology," while the "parallels we draw between machines and living things strongly color our understanding of the world," nowadays, since information is so central to biology, "life is thought of as a genetic code, and like a machine is available for editing" (89).

The question of how best to categorize bodies (whether they be human, post-human, clone, or other) matters a great deal, yet there is no way to do so without first considering the legal/juridical practices of the time in question, a point that Margrit Shildrick makes in her article "Transgressing the Law with Foucault and Derrida: Some Reflections on Anomalous Embodiment." As part of her discussion of beings that transgress boundaries, she contends that "transgressive bodily form matters primarily in view of its impact on a series of established regulations setting out what is proper to a particular moment in socio-cultural history," thus highlighting how the legal status of bodies must always must be viewed within a particular context (Shildrick 30).

To be sure, as beings, humans have traditionally been understood not only in relation to others, but also within a specific cultural and historical framework. Indeed, just as Amélie Oksenberg Rorty explains in her article "A Literary Postscript: Characters, Persons, Selves, Individuals," the concept of "a person is not something that stands still, hospitably waiting an analysis of its necessary and sufficient conditions" (301). These definitions "change historically, forced by changes in social conditions and in answer to one another's weighty inconsistencies" (Rorty 301).

N. Katherine Hayles, who also addresses this subject, emphasizes in her book *How We Became Post-Human: Virtual Bodies in Cybernetics, Literature, and Informatics*, that the way we view the status of bodies hinges largely "on whether the being in question has been manufactured of born" (163). In other words, beings can be either born or "built." Given this particular criteria, clones trouble the already fragile boundaries between human and other in terms of their origin. The clones that populate the film's narrative have, in fact, been created via a process of manufacturing. Moreover, the biotechnology corporation that has created them describes these clones to their prospective clients as nothing more than products.

Yet, even given these perspectives, there remain lingering questions regarding the clones' ontological status. In the film, it is difficult to distinguish human from clone (since the clones share many traits in common with the humans they were copied from). Added to this, the fact remains that the film depicts clones as achieving self-awareness and even, at least in the case of protagonists Lincoln Six Echo (played by Ewan McGregor) and Jordan Two Delta (played by Scarlett Johannson), questioning and then ultimately coming to terms with their situation. Therefore—in Cartesian terms, at least—both Lincoln Six Echo and Jordan Two Delta have demonstrated enough awareness to be deserving of basic human rights.

Complicating matters, the clones—when necessary—are able to "pass" as human without much difficulty. For example, when Lincoln Six Echo and Jordan Two Delta escape the compound, they are able to freely navigate the outside world without arousing much suspicion. Moreover, Lincoln Six Echo is persuasive when he, late in the film, impersonates the human he was copied from.

Even further confounding matters, it comes to light that Lincoln Six Echo apparently shares some memories with the original human from whom he has been cloned. These memories are latent and at first only appear to him in the form of dreams, which he interprets as nightmares. He describes to Dr. Merrick, one of the doctors in charge of the compound, how he frequently dreams that he is aboard a beautiful boat. On the same piece of paper where he sketches the boat for Dr. Merrick, Lincoln writes the word "Renovatio," confiding that while he does not know what the word means, it frequently appears in his dreams (the term "renovatio," in fact, refers to "re-birth"). It is later revealed that Tom Lincoln (also played by McGregor), the human from whom Lincoln Six Echo was copied, has made a fortune by designing cutting edge boats and motorcycles, thus raising questions about the connection between the two. Could Tom Lincoln have passed his engineering skills and design prowess on to his clone? Might Lincoln Six Echo possess some of his original's memories?

Not only do these dreams link clone and original, making it all the more difficult to distinguish between the two, but they also bring up complex questions related to the relationship between memories and identity. Recall the position of John Locke (1632–1704), who claimed that memories of our past help us construct our sense of identity and self (Locke is discussed in more detail in the chapter devoted to Lafferty's novel, *Six Wakes*). To an extent, person-hood means having psychological continuity, according to Locke's view, since he considered personal identity to be founded on consciousness (memory). As the "psychological continuity theorists," who updated and slightly revised Locke's theories suggest, the culmination of personal memories help to make individuals who they are.

Indeed, even today, there is little dispute in the psychological community that, as humans, our memories and experiences help shape who we are. Scientists have gone as far as to argue that people "are their memories," a point that Abby Smith Rumsey underscores in her 2016 book *What When We Are No More: How Digital Memory Is Shaping Our Future*. Indeed, memories are "the very fabric of the self, woven of experiences, endowing us with time, place, personality, and identity in the world" (Rumsey).

Beyond provoking questions about the relationship between memories and the self, Lincoln Six Echo's dreams also foreshadow his eventual face-to-face meeting with Tom Lincoln, an encounter which bring issues related to identity to the forefront. Not only does the meeting of the two doppelgangers portend death (thus hearkening back to early iterations of the motif of the double), but it also invokes traditional themes such as the fear of the self and the search for the identity. Significantly, alongside these concerns, the meeting between Lincoln Six Echo and Tom Lincoln also speaks to contemporary debates about the limits—ethical and otherwise—of biotechnology.

The fateful meeting between the two men—who are doubles and look identical to one another—happens after Lincoln Six Echo, accompanied by his friend and fellow clone, Jordan Two Delta, flees to Tom Lincoln's house seeking asylum and answers. While Tom initially behaves hostilely toward Lincoln Six Echo by attacking him (in what, admittedly, could be construed as self-defense), he later acts friendly and rather matter-of-factly inquires what Lincoln wants. Lincoln and Jordan, fearing for their own safety and also in attempt to save the other clones, plead with Tom for help. They want him to stand with them in opposition to the biotechnology corporation that runs the cloning facility.

Tom says that he will help them, but he ends up betraying them by contacting Dr. Merrick and telling him that he found his clone. This encounter not only positions clone against human, but it also highlights the differences between the two. For all they share in common, much separates Lincoln Six Echo from Tom Lincoln, who is aggressive and lacks honor. Unlike his clone (who is loyal to his friends and has compassion for others), Tom Lincoln shows that he has no problem betraying others. Yet, though Lincoln Six Echo clearly possesses admirable traits that his human counterpart lacks, he does not have the same basic rights that have been afforded to the human original.

Nonetheless, the fact that Lincoln and Tom look identical works to the clone's advantage. After the betrayal comes to light, the two get into quite a scuffle. Tom does not want to kill his clone until a replacement can be made (he wants to hold onto his "insurance policy"), so holds Lincoln Six Echo at gunpoint until he can be taken back to the facility. This plan backfires, though, because once reinforcements from the compound arrive, they cannot tell them apart. Lincoln Six Echo uses the moment of confusion to his advantage and slips his clone watch on Tom Lincoln's wrist, a move which successfully tricks Mr. Laurent, a member of the security detail, into shooting Tom (since Laurent mistakenly believes him to be the clone).

With the death of Tom Lincoln, *The Island* echoes a pattern that has long been associated with the figure of the doppelganger. For Tom Lincoln, seeing his double indeed has been a bad omen, and their face-to-face encounter does lead to his demise. Thus, with the addition of this plot detail, the film reflects how the figure has traditionally appeared in storylines. Moreover, the film hearkens back to the notion of the "uncanny," a concept which has traditionally been associated with the double.

O'Riordan discusses the relationship between the uncanny and the film's representations of doppelgangers, but clarifies that "issues of twinning, copying, and the uncanny" only come "into play late in the film narrative when the cloned characters discover that they are clones, and the clients appear on screen, through images such as the bill board advertisement image" (154). One result of this deferred meeting is that viewers tend to sympathize with the clones' predicament, since they encounter them first. Indeed, "the primacy of the characters of the clones (over the clients) is gained through this narrative ordering" (O'Riordan 154).

The film's ultimate stance is one decidedly in favor of the clones deserving human rights. *The Island*, however, fails to resolve many of the dilemmas it introduces and the film also never fully addresses questions it has raised about the status of the clones. Indeed, rather than answering the many complex questions raised throughout the narrative, the film ends by blurring categories. Nonetheless, it stops short of fully dissolving the boundaries between human and clone. This results in the film ending on an ambivalent note.

Yet, despite this uncertain ending, *The Island* works well not only as a cautionary tale about the ethics of cloning, but also as a critique of the commodification of biotechnology and a (more general) warning about the dangers of science run amuck. The film also, both implicitly and explicitly, challenges the notion that science and technology can solve the many problems that humanity faces. Yet the film, also, especially through its representations of clones, reflects 21st century cultural anxieties related to the relationship between identity and technology.

Clones in *Oblivion*

Similar to *The Island*, the plot of *Oblivion* centers on clones who have been kept in the dark about both their nature and purpose. In both films, a storyline about clones coming to terms with the reality of their existence takes center stage. Like in *The Island* (and so many other storylines that involve clones), *Oblivion* thus raises questions about the nature of clones and about the ethics of human cloning while also provoking contemporary cultural anxieties. However, while the central conflict in *The Island* is between clone and human, the antagonists of *Oblivion* turn out to be an alien race which has created human clones for their own nefarious purposes.

Set in 2077, *Oblivion* imagines a largely uninhabited Earth, recently devastated by a war with hostile aliens. The majority of the human survivors have been relocated to Titan, a Saturn moon. Jack Harper (played by Tom Cruise), the film's protagonist, has stayed on Earth as part of a skeleton crew charged with completing repairs. Harper, along with his colleague and love interest Victoria/Vika (played by Andrea Riseborough), reside together in a tower in close orbit to the Earth. As Nick Jones explains it his review of the film, the early parts of the narrative make it seem like these are "the last two people left alive on Earth" (Jones 290).

They have been led believe they have just a few weeks left on the planet before they, too, will join their fellow human survivors on the extraterrestrial colony. Although Jack Harper has been pushed to believe that his mission is simple enough, he has been having strange dreams that suggest otherwise. These dreams feature a mysterious woman who he is drawn to for reasons he can neither comprehend nor explain. Complicating matters, Jack has recently undergone a "mandatory memory wipe," and is apparently suffering from some sort of amnesia.

During what begins as a routine work day, Harper comes across a beautiful woman named Julia (played Olga Kurylenko), an apparent survivor of a downed spacecraft; she reminds Jack of the woman from his dreams, so he takes her back to the tower he shares with Vika. When the two return, however, Vika is not happy to see a woman with Jack so she refuses them entry and reports them; this results in a drone being launched, which targets their location. In the resulting attack, Vika gets killed but Jack and Julia manage to escape.

Jack and Julia, who have taken refuge on the planet's surface, come across another ship. It is being tended to by a technician, who, much to Jack's dismay, looks identical to him. It turns out that this tech is actually a clone of Jack and the two end up fighting. Confronted with this startling discovery, Jack goes on a mission to find answers. He soon learns that hostile extraterrestrials are responsible for decimating Earth and that they cloned the human astronauts with whom—decades ago, it turns out—they made first orbital contact (he finds a flight recording which confirms this theory). Jack and Vika were members of this crew, along with Julia (who, in turns out, was married to Jack at the time). The film ends after one of the Jack clones chooses to sacrifice himself to destroy the aliens—thus enacting a form of vengeance up the hostile invaders. His sacrifice also saves Julia.

As this description suggests, *Oblivion* recalls a number of other science fiction texts in terms of its plot and reliance on generic formulas made popular by science fiction film and literature—not to mention in its treatment of clones. Additionally, the setting of *Oblivion*—a post-apocalyptic Earth—is one commonly used in the science fiction genre. Indeed, just as Ryan Lamble highlights in his review of the film, "there is much in *Oblivion*'s story and plot twists that is familiar from other sci-fi touchstones." This includes the fact that Jack Harper is a clone—a plot detail which Lamble says likens the film to Duncan Jones's *Moon*, which "itself follows a genre staple that stretches back to Aldous Huxley's *Brave New World*."

Beyond relying on the trope of clones, the film also echoes other recent science fiction films in its representation of showing survivors on a post-apocalyptic Earth. To be sure, since the late 20th century, there has been a near-exhaustive list of science fiction films set on a dystopian Earth. As Christopher Holliday, writing for *Science Fiction Film and Television*, summarizes the situation:

> The devastation wrought upon a ravaged and ruined Planet Earth, one that is no longer fit for satisfactory human habitation, has emerged as the common currency of much contemporary SF cinema. From *Twelve Monkeys* (Gilliam US 1995), *28 Days Later* (Boyle UK 2002) and *I Am Legend* (Lawrence US 2007) to *The Book of Eli* (the Hughes Brothers US 2010), *After Earth* (Shyamalan US 2013), *World War Z* (Forster US/Malta 2013) and *Oblivion* (Kosinski US 2013), the number of films trading in the terminal destruction of humanity has proliferated [433].

The commonality these films share is how they represent "dystopian versions of the future in which human freedom and social community are seriously disrupted," a point that John Hoben makes in "Reading Alien Suns" (106). Indeed, Kosinski's *Oblivion* follows this tradition due to its post-apocalyptic setting and focus on the apparent survivors of this catastrophe. Yet, while *Oblivion* clearly fits into this tradition of dystopian film, it remains concerned with much more than dramatically rendering a ruined Earth.

Indeed, much like *The Island*, *Oblivion* is a clone narrative which explores the relationship between memory and identity. Moreover, because *Oblivion* represents futuristic technology in a negative light, the film also calls attention to the perils of scientific progress and its potentially dehumanizing effects. Paradoxically, however, Jack Harper, the film's protagonist, ends up relying on (yet another form of) technology to help him piece his memories together, so *Oblivion*, like so many of the other texts discussed, ends on a rather ambivalent note with respect to technology's role. Finally, especially in the way the film ends, *Oblivion* also proves to be timely in terms of its representation of warfare in a post–9/11 globalized society.

As a clone narrative that also remains invested in exploring the relationship between memory and identity, *Oblivion* uses the presence of (a veritable army of) clones to raise provocative questions. The film imagines hostile aliens who have the technological ability to clone humans. Rather than portraying cloning as an enhancement to the human condition, these clones are depicted as particularly susceptible to exploitation since the same aliens who created them have also discovered a way to effectively wipe their memories. The aliens have, in the words of Nick Jones, found a way to "integrate humanity into systems of exploitation," therefore milking humans of their "labor power … through rigorous indoctrination," which culminates in the human clones becoming "willing participants" in their own destruction (291–292).

Although Jack Harper has been indoctrinated in this very manner, he "wakes up over the course of the film to the scope of technology's influence on his life and thoughts" (Jones 290). It is his memories, which come to him at first in the form of dreams, which bring him newfound awareness about his situation. Joana Catarina de Sousa Caetano discusses the role Jack's dreams play in "Memories are Forever: Transhumanism and Cultural Memory in *V for Vendetta*, *Oblivion*, and *The Giver*." In that article, she explains that clone Jack's dreams,

> are, in fact, Commander Jack Harper's original memories. Drawing on immediate perceptions and flashbacks, Jack the clone pushes his brain to its limits in order to understand the meaning of these images that are memories of Commander Jack and his wife at the top of the Empire State building in pre-war times. Jack the clone believes these images are dreams because five years have passed since the mandatory memory wipe and all life before then should have vanished, and yet … he questions … he wonders [de Sousa Caetano 34].

One reason that clone Jack has difficulty reconciling these memories is that they contradict so much of what he has been conditioned to believe. Moreover, though he does share some memories of the past with his original, he has also had recent experiences which are his own. Thus, he must resolve these early memories with his own recollections.

Far from being troubled by the past, Jack Harper, instead, seems to look back with nostalgia. As Todd McCarthy points out in his discussion of the film, "Jack seems to relish being haunted by the past" (108). Indeed, in one scene, he "nostalgically wallows in lore surrounding the final Super Bowl, played in 2017, while standing among the ruins of the stadium where it took place, and uses the upper part of the Empire State Building, which sticks out of the ground that has swallowed the rest of the structure, as a sort of home base and control tower" (McCarthy 108). Claire Colebrook, who in her essay "Time That Is Intolerant" also discusses nostalgia as it relates to the film, notes that *Oblivion*'s central character "lives in a depleted world, but manages to onto the past" (148). In this manner, the film relies on Jack's nostalgia to look back longingly to the past—and as a way to raise concerns about the future. It also calls into questions the need for so much technological progress.

Indeed, as several of the film's critics and reviewers have been quick to point out, the film functions as a cautionary tale, not just about the ethics of cloning, but also about the perils that so-called progress can bring. As Nick Jones highlights, "*Oblivion* is a polished, overtly precision-engineered production about the danger of precision-engineered products" (290). Moreover, especially in the way the film ends, *Oblivion* "admits the ambivalence that should by rights accompany any merging of humanity and technology" (Jones 290).

To be sure, the film presents a complicated stance on technology, in part, due to the way that it both enslaves and liberates its protagonist, Jack Harper, and his fellow human clones. There is little doubt that the extra-terrestrial technology—which is used to create the army of clones—aims to enslave humans to make them carry out work for the hostile aliens. In this sense, technology proves to be de-humanizing. Given this set of circumstances, clones in *Oblivion* exist solely to serve their alien masters.

While technology has succeeded in largely stripping Jack of both his identity and humanity, it is, ironically, also the means which restores that which he so clearly values. Indeed, his search for self finally gets fulfilled when he finds the flight recording which confirms his theory that he has been copied from a heroic human astronaut. *Oblivion* thus suggests that technology also has the potential to empower the individual, which is what happens when Jack Harper gets much-needed answers from the shuttle's flight recording.

Although for his part Jack seems largely satisfied with this discovery, the film nonetheless ends on an ambivalent note with respect to the role technology plays in uncovering identity. The recording, which Jack prizes as the key to learning about himself, functions as what Alison Landsberg calls an example of a "prosthetic memory," a concept she first described in 1994 in "Prosthetic Memory: *Total Recall* and *Blade Runner*." As Landsberg explains, "by prosthetic memories I mean memories which do not come from a person's lived experience in any strict sense" (175).

Landsberg refines and further develops this concept in her later study, *Prosthetic Memory: The Transformation of American Remembrance in the Age of Mass Culture* (2004), a book where she discusses how memories can be transmitted culturally. The result is that a person who is experiencing, per se, these types of memories has no first-hand experience of the actual event in question. This could occur, for instance, if a person were to view a film or television program and then form a memory of the narrative events which transpired (without actually having actually experienced those events in any manner). The same experience could also occur when a person sees a photograph or hears a recording.

Indeed, in *Oblivion* the recording that clone Jack finds provides him with the exact type of memory that Alison Lansberg describes. In truth, of course, it was not clone Jack who made the recording—it was Commander Jack Harper (the human he was cloned from)—nor does clone Jack actually have any first-hand memories of making the recording. Instead, they were made by another Jack and then preserved—and only later communicated to him, via this form of technology. Nonetheless, clone Jack chooses to accept the recording as valid.

As Landsberg argues, prosthetic memories also work to produce empathy and social responsibility. In the case of clone Jack, these feeling culminate in his decision to sacrifice himself in the film's conclusion. Indeed, clone Jack, armed with this newfound self-awareness (which he gets from the recording he recovered), chooses to emulate his human predecessor and thus proceeds to weaponize his shuttle in order to destroy the aliens and save Julia and the remaining human clones who are on Earth. This final scene not only serves to showcase the role prosthetic memories play in the film, but it also underscores how *Oblivion* remains very much the product of the 21st century.

To be clear, especially with respect to its conclusion, the film reveals itself to be a product of a globalized, post–9/11 America, particularly through Jack Harper's use of "unconventional tactics—turning droids into improvised explosive devices, and eventually, a suicide bombing—to bring this inhuman war machine's reign to an end" (Lamble). As Lamble highlights, this is just one of the parallels between *Oblivion*'s events and recent global conflicts (such as in Iraq), which have been characterized by this type of warfare and the presence of weaponized drones. As Elizabeth Haas, Terry Christensen, and Peter J. Haas argue in their book *Projecting Politics: Political Messages in American Film*, it is not mere coincidence that *Oblivion*, which they situate as part of the "disaster film genre," was made amidst the confluence of government dysfunction and "shifting military deployments." To be sure, *Oblivion*'s plot echoes current events, while it also calls attention to cultural anxieties about the relationship between identity, memory, and technology.

Clones in Cinema: Reflections on Memory, Identity and Technology

Indeed, as a science fiction film that relies on the doppelganger motif through representations of human clones, *Oblivion* showcases how the figure can function as a cultural vehicle to shine a light on recent events as well as to call attention contemporary anxieties about identity in the face of emerging technologies. Similarly, *The Island* also provokes current controversies through its portrayal of clones, which, in much the same fashion, reflects ambivalence about emerging biotechnologies.

The Island indeed proves to be a timely and relevant film, especially because of the way its plot raises questions about the limits—ethical and other—of science. In the same manner, *Oblivion* also responds to current debates while also serving as a cautionary tale about the de-humanizing potential of technology. Beyond addressing these ethical issues, both films interrogate the relationship between memory and identity while also testing boundaries with their representations of clones—particularly in the way that clones from both films (quite inexplicably) retain the memories of their human counterparts. To be sure, both *The Island* and *Oblivion* trouble, at the same time as they highlight concerns about, the concept of identity—a concept which is being challenged in response to the advent of new technologies.

12. Monstrous Doubling and Magical Illusion in *The Prestige*

"Every great magic trick consists of three acts. The first act is called 'the pledge'—the magician shows you something ordinary, but of course, it probably isn't. The second act is called 'the turn'—the magician makes this ordinary something do something extraordinary. Now you're looking for the secret ... but you won't find it. That's why there's a third act called 'the prestige'—it's the part with the twists and turn."—Christopher Nolan, *The Prestige*

A film which features two sets of doubles, *The Prestige* (2006) is a mystery-thriller directed by Christopher Nolan. Together with his brother Jonathan Nolan, Christopher Nolan wrote the screenplay for the film based on Christopher Priest's 1995 novel of the same name. The story, which begins in London at the end of the 19th century, follows competing stage magicians Robert Angier (played by Hugh Jackman) and Alfred Borden (played by Christian Bale), men who were once friends and colleagues, but turn into bitter rivals when Angier's wife Julia dies in a tragic stage accident.

Julia McCullough (played by Piper Perabo) worked as magician's assistant to an illusionist named Milton (played by Rickey Jay) and she appeared on stage as part of his magic show. One night she was performing a water cell trick with her husband Robert and the other assistant, Alfred Borden, when something went terribly wrong. Just prior to this fateful night, Borden has suggested using a different kind of knot for the act, but was advised against it. When performing the act onstage that night, Julia found herself unable to get loose from the ropes. Realizing too late that she was in distress, the men watched on helplessly as Julia drowned on stage in front of a live audience. Angier, believing that Borden tied too tight of a knot in the ropes that bound Julia, blamed him for her death. Thus began the feud between Angier and Borden.

12. Monstrous Doubling and Magical Illusion in The Prestige

Much of the plot of *The Prestige* revolves around the men's ensuing rivalry. The movie follows both Robert Angier (who performs as "The Great Danton") and Alfred Borden (who appears onstage as "The Professor") as they gain recognition as stage magicians in London. For these stage magicians, however, fame comes at a high personal cost. The men work tirelessly to one-up each other by performing a series of dangerous illusions on stage—ultimately culminating with both Angier and Borden performing a variation of an act called the "Transported Man." However, while they are celebrated for their performances, the men end up suffering many personal losses. The rivalry thus pushes the men to become better magicians, but their feud also takes a high personal toll on them both.

As Ann Heilmann, who discusses the film as part of her article "Doing It with Mirrors: Neo-Victorian Metatextual Magic in *Affinity*, *The Prestige*, and *The Illusionist*," explains, this rivalry, "the leitmotif of *The Prestige*, is here a phase in the magician's evolution" (37). For much of the movie, Angier strives to emulate Borden's spectacular version of the "Transported Man" trick, where he disappears and reappears instantaneously on the other side of the stage. Eventually, Angier manages to not only match Borden, but to surpass him.

While the rivalry between Angier and Borden takes the shape of each man vying to be the better stage magician, at its core, their dispute revolves around anxieties about identity, which is also the film's principle conceit. Film scholars, as well as a number of reviewers, have noted this theme. For instance, as it is explained in a discussion of the film that appears in *Indie Wire*, "while each man has his own double subplot, perhaps the most interesting meta-theme is how these great rivals mirror each other too, [which is] especially reflected in their obsessive but callous relationships with their wives and lovers (Piper Perabo, Rebecca Hall and Scarlett Johansson)." Daniel Cojocaru also addresses this theme in his article "Man's Desire Exceeds His Grasp—*The Prestige* as Utopia," where he offers a reading of the film which relies upon René Girard's mimetic theory. He explains that their rivalry can best be

> understood as what Chesterton calls "the greatest difficulty of man," when one considers it in terms of René Girard's mimetic theory. In *I See Satan Fall like Lightning*, Girard uncovers the problem of human desire in the Tenth Commandment's interdiction of coveting what belongs to one's neighbor. His anthropological model revolves around the tenet that human beings desire what belongs to one's neighbor because of a lack of autonomous identity. The object that belongs to one's neighbor seems desirable because the other seems to possess an identity that the self is lacking. Hence it is not so much the object that is being desired but the very being of the person possessing the object [Cojocaru].

As evidence that this need to establish identity is what motivates Angier and Borden, as well as fuels their feud, Cojocaru stresses how the "magicians obtain possession of their rival's diary and discover their imitative desire for the other's being" (Cojocaru). According to Todd McGowan, who analyzes the film in his article "The Violence of Creation in *The Prestige*," it is indeed this desire which also pushes the men to keep "secrets and punish each other in what becomes an increasingly vicious feud that results in multiple deaths and much unnecessary suffering. Due to their determination to be the better magician and to simultaneously destroy the other, they each lose their wives to tragic deaths and finally die themselves as a direct result of their rivalry" (McGowan 1).

Angier feels that, between the two, he is the better showman, so he cannot understand why Borden draws a larger audience, nor can he comprehend how Borden manages to so convincingly pull off the "Transported Man" trick. Eventually Angier grows so desperate to learn Borden's secrets that he arranges to steal his rival's diary. He pores over the journal's pages in the hopes of discovering his rival's secrets; his search is fruitless, however, because what he is reading is actually a decoy diary (planted to confuse and misdirect Angier). While the decoy diary works to drive Angier temporarily out of London, it does not stop his obsession.

On the contrary, it drives him to Colorado Springs where he finds Nikola Tesla (played by David Bowie), the famous inventor, and convinces him to create a duplicating machine for him. While Angier still does not know Borden's secrets, the new technology he procures enables him to perform his own version of the "Transported Man," one which not only rivals but actually surpasses Borden's. As Rupert Read explains in his article "The Tale Parfit Tells: Analytic Metaphysics of Personal Identity vs. Wittgensteinian Film and Literature," Angier, "to equal and better Borden, eventually gets hold of an actual teletransporter. This allows him to move from one side of the theater to the other instantaneously. But there is a catch: When the teletransporter fires off, it leaves him also, or, if you prefer, a duplicate/replica of him, inside the teletransporter" (131). Having perfected his stage trick, thanks to this machine, Angier returns to London. Every night, as part of his show, Angier creates and then kills clones of himself.

While Robert Angier relies on technology to perform his version of the "Transported Man," Alfred Borden is able to pull off his stage act because he is actually two people: two twins pretending to be one person. Late in the film, he admits that pulling off this trick was "simple, maybe, but not easy," because it required so much sacrifice. In order to protect their secret, the two siblings took turns playing both Borden and Fallon, his servant (Bale was not only acting the part of the two twins, but he also played the role of Fallon). One brother loved a woman named Sarah (played by Rebecca Hall) and they eventually marry and have a daughter. The other Borden twin loved Olivia (played by Scarlett Johansson), but he had to hide his relationship with her from the world, since it would have appeared that the two were having an extramarital affair—and, indeed, Borden's wife comes to believe that her husband is being unfaithful to her. In actuality, however, each man was faithful to his respective lover. Neither woman, however, was able to cope with life with Borden. In the end, Sarah tragically commits suicide and Olivia decides to break it off with him.

Despite the high cost of maintaining this façade, pretending to be one person has also opened many doors for Borden by enabling him to perform different magic tricks, such as (most strikingly) the "Transported Man" act in which he appears to move instantaneously from the stage to the other side of the theater. It also gives him the element of surprise (which he needs) when, very late in the film, one twin, the other having been publically executed after being framed for murder, confronts and then kills Angier, thus exacting ultimate vengeance. Indeed, it is not until this final scene that Angier learns the truth about Borden.

Monstrous Magic

Certainly, both men have secrets that they carry with them until the final moments of the film. Indeed, when the truth about both Borden and Angier gets revealed, viewers learn much not only about these magicians' "magic," but the audience also discovers the film's sleight of hand. In the end, Borden and Angier, magicians who for so much of the film have been the subject of spectacle, prove to be monstrous, as well. In fact, the film quite deliberately conflates magic with the monstrous.

The film's main characters are individuals who perform magic and illusions, types of entertainment that have for so long been associated with monstrosity. Performing magic—whether entertaining with illusions or stage tricks—is of the oldest performing arts in the world, and until the 18th century, magic shows were commonly found as part of a traveling troupe or in conjunction with a fair. Itinerant performers would entertain the public with magic tricks and traditional spectacles such as juggling, sword swallowing, and fire-breathing. Beginning in the 18th century, however, performing magic became more mainstream, so performances began be held for private patrons. Soon thereafter, what is now known as modern stage magic became popular. In 1840, John Henry Anderson (1814–1874) opened the New Strand Theatre in London. Around the same time (in 1845), Jean Eugène Robert-Houdin (1805–1871) opened a magic theater in Paris. In their respective venues, these men transformed magic into a spectacle the general public could pay to see live on stage. During the latter half of the 19th century, the popularity of these types of stage magic shows grew, and, consequently, larger scale magic shows permanently staged at big theater venues became commonplace.

Going back to its origins, magic shows have long been considered a form a public spectacle—and this remained the case well in the 19th and even earlier 20th centuries, the time periods which inspired the film's depictions of stage magic. As Christian Bailly describes the scene, "myriad spectacles were offered to the nineteenth-century public. Acrobats and magicians held crowds spellbound with their performances" (20). Both magic shows and their cousin, "the notorious freak shows of the nineteenth and early twentieth centuries, intended to be public spectacle," a point that Elaine L. Graham notes (39). As such, their success or failure largely depended on the crowd they drew—and upon the crowd's response. In *The Prestige*, these same type of spectacles can be seen, but in the film, rather than featuring illusionists who pretend to perform magic (which is, of course, what real-life stage magicians do), these performers move beyond illusion into the realm of the monstrous.

The term "monster" has an interesting etymology, one which sheds light on the nature of both Alfred Borden and Robert Angier as they are depicted in the film. As Edward J. Ingebretsen asserts in his article "Staking the Monster: A Politics of Remonstrance," the "*monstrum* was that wonder-making person or event" (94). He further explains: "Originally applied to birth abnormalities, the term gradually widened to include a range of the anomalous and humanly unusual. Ironically enough, this taxonomic movement accompanied or perhaps facilitated an increasingly narrow shaping of the 'human'" (Ingebretsen 94). Monsters, simply put, are that which transgress boundaries, which is precisely what both Borden and Angier do in *The Prestige* in order to convincingly pull off their stage illusions.

As Terry Kirk describes in the article "Monumental Monstrosity, Monstrous Monumentally," "Monsters are deviant, transgressive, threatening, and therefore horrible, terrifying, and tremendous yet also astonishing, marvelous, and prodigious. The modern scientist orders monsters in terms of relationships to nature's norms. Paré classified them as either prodigious apparitions beyond the course of nature or deviant creations entirely against its course" (7). This description of monsters fits Borden and Angier perfectly. Both are simultaneously marvelous and terrifying for what they can do onstage. Both also transgress natural boundaries as they have traditionally been understood because of what they are.

In Borden's case, his stage success rests on the fact that he is actually two men (twin brothers) who share an identity and therefore the same life. He is transgressive in this respect, both because of what he does—which is practice deception by pretending to be one person when he is actually two—and because of what he is: a twin. Going back historically, twins have long been viewed as anomalous and even monstrous. Indeed, for centuries, the birth of twins was "regarded as unnatural and monstrous" in many different cultures (Schapera 117). The birth of twins has also long-been the subject of much fascination and speculation. As V. Dasen explains in "Multiple Births in Ancient Medical Texts," ancient medical writers and biologists would elaborate different theories to explain the phenomenon of twins and multiple births. One route to the monstrous is, indeed, through "monstrous births"—and, for centuries, the birth of twins could thus be categorized, a point that Marie Hélène Huet emphasizes in her book *Monstrous Imagination*, as part of her discussion "monstrous progeny" and "monstrous births" (1;14). Historically, "monstrosities challenged the general laws of procreation," and were therefore seen as transgressive (Huet 14). Monstrous births were threatening and provoked anxieties precisely because of the way they troubled boundaries. Indeed, monsters prove to be "worse than debilitating disease; they are disquieting miscreations of ourselves. All humans begin their existence not as perfect predetermined beings but as vulnerable embryos and potential monsters" (Kirk 7).

Speaking about both Borden and Angier, these men veer into the realm of the monstrous because of the way they test the boundaries between human and other. They are also monstrous because of the anxieties their existence provokes. Zakiya Hanafi goes as far as to argue in her book *The Monster in the Machine: Magic, Medicine, and the Marvelous in the Time of the Scientific Revolution*, that "we stake out the boundaries of our humanity by delineating the boundaries of the monstrous." Thus, the "human and the monster vie for space between two thresholds" (Hanafi). This conflict is the source of anxiety because of the way it calls into question human nature. As Graham emphasizes, monsters signal "a terrible breach in formerly inviolate categories" (Graham 39). Both Borden and Angier are monstrous in this sense. They trouble the very boundaries that they transgress. As Graham explains, this is the meaning of monsters: "Monsters have a double function, therefore, simultaneously marking the boundaries between the normal and the pathological but also exposing the fragility of the very taken-for-grantedness of such categories" (39).

In Angier's case, the root of his monstrosity stems from his relationship with technology. His monstrous magic is actually the result of a monstrous machine, which allows him to duplicate himself. Indeed, unlike Borden, who pulls of the "Transported Man" trick because there are actually two men (twins) in on the act, Angier uses technology—specifically Tesla's duplicating machine—to make copies of himself so that he can perfect his stage performance. This depiction of "magic" speaks to 21st century anxieties about technology and its potentially devastating effects while also hearkening back to fears that came about during the scientific revolution.

Speaking of the scientific revolution, Hanafi notes that "machine-like and monstrous are synonymous in this period." Indeed, during this time period, humanity was threatened by emerging technologies which offered so much potential but also foretold danger. New machines also cast a shadow on how humans saw themselves: "Just as the nonhuman, or the monstrous, became associated with autonomously powered machines, so the human body, likened to a machine, became monstrous in its own eyes" (Hanafi). This same anxiety is reflected by Angier's use of the duplicating machine, which grants him the success on stage that he has dreamed of, but it comes at such a high cost. Although to a contemporary crowd, "a clear distinction can be made between 'magic' and 'science' of the Western variety," this was not the case in centuries past (Wax and Wax 495). Hence, Angier's act also conflates "magic" with "science," since it is a form of technology (a machine) which allows him to pull off his stage trick.

To be sure, in *The Prestige*, magic is consistently portrayed as monstrous. Since in the film the magicians are the ones with doppelgangers (who allow them to so skillfully perform their illusions on stage), this fact also works to highlight the potentially troubling nature of the doppelganger. The film repeatedly suggests there is a horror associated with doubling, a point that Read emphasizes: "*The Prestige* expertly explores the horror, the terrible turn in events, that may follow from duplication, not merely of hats but of human beings (specifically of Angier, and in a way, of course, of Borden, too)" (134).

Identity, Nature and Technology

Without a doubt, *The Prestige* is more than just a movie about magicians vying to have the better stage show. For one, the film proves to be an important cultural product because of how it treats questions related to identity. The film also noticeably provokes 21st century cultural tensions by positioning technology as at odds with the natural world, and, indeed, the film works to underscore the fact that not all technology brings about beneficial change. The film thus calls into question the notion that technology brings about an enhancement to the human condition.

While the film calls into question the beneficial nature of technology, it also does much to show nature as being at odds with technology. As characters, the Borden twins and Angier and his many clones (all of whom were created by Tesla's duplicating machine), showcase this friction, since the Borden twins represent nature (and its monstrous potential) while Angier and his many doppelgangers symbolize the power and danger of technology (which can also prove monstrous). These tensions resonate with a 21st century audience for good reason. Between reproductive technologies (such as cloning and IVF, which is, in essence, a way to create twins through science) and machines which permit duplication and transmission (such as the many types of machines which permit copying, faxing, scanning, and, more recently, 3-D printing), those of us living in the 21st century are besieged with new technologies, many of which involve duplication of some sort.

While these emerging technologies may promise to be beneficial tools, they also provoke anxieties by threatening to go beyond the (so-called) natural order of things. To be sure, though the availability of these new tools offers clear benefits (they can be convenient, improve productivity, and many of these machines even have medical applications), they also threaten tradition, pushing some to believe that these (so-called) advancements come at too high a cost. The film *The Prestige* responds directly to the advent of these new tools. Indeed, by representing the duplication of a person, the film raises troubling and provocative questions about the limits—ethical and scientific, alike—of creating new types of machines since their very existence promises to augment, if not altogether dissolve, the binaries between human and other.

The Conceit of Doubling

As Will Brooker, who discusses the film in "Are You Watching Closely?" points out, doubles "haunt Nolan's movies, and resonate across his work as a whole" (xii). *The Prestige* does not simply include treatment of doubles, but, as Brooker notes, it is a film "built around a structure of twins and clones" (Brooker xii). Indeed, as Read emphasizes, the film works a "marvelous meditation on human doubling" (130). Indeed, the fact that the film relies so heavily upon both twins and clones as part of its plot bears scrutiny. For one, it shows how *The Prestige* is yet another example of a recent film which features doppelgangers. In *The Prestige*, however, the presence of twins resonates quite differently than the existence of clones, due to what each represents as well as because of the questions each raises about origins.

Twins, of course, occur in nature—and they have been around as long as there have been human beings—but they have frequently been associated with superstition and have also been viewed as a source of either fascination or horror. As Dasen explains, in ancient times, there was much discussion by medical writers and early biologists who likened multiple births to monstrosity and animality. To be sure, as I. Schapera notes, the birth of twins has been known to rouse "every possible form of emotion, from extreme terror to heartfelt joy. This is especially marked among primitive peoples, where the emotion is translated into action, and where the reaction produced by the birth of twins almost invariably differs from that produced by normal birth" (117). As he further asserts, sometimes the twins are "regarded as unnatural and monstrous, and therefore as portending evil. The unfortunate children, and perhaps also their mother, are looked upon as guilty of a serious crime, a crime calculated to call down the vengeance of the higher powers" (Schapera 117).

In *The Prestige*, part of the mystery of illusion relies upon the existence of twins since neither Angier nor the crowds that gather to watch Borden's "Transported Man" trick (nor even the film's audience!) initially understands that Borden is actually two men, a fact which he exploits to create his stage illusion. For his part, Angier cannot figure out how Borden pulls off the trick either. In response to Borden's stage act—and in a desperate bid to best Borden—Angier eventually acquires an actual teletransporter, which allows him to move from the stage to the other side of the theater instantaneously.

Tesla's machine, however, is not what it first appears to be. Each time Angier steps inside the teletransporter, it leaves one version of him inside the machine and simultaneously transports another version (a duplicate or replica) across the room. Thus, the machine is, in effect, making clones of Angier. As part of his analysis of the film, Read claims that, due to this plot point, *The Prestige* offers a compelling dramatization of what he calls the "tale Parfit tells," since the machine creates what Parfit refers to as a "branch-line case" (129). Derek Parfit (1942–2017) was a British philosopher and ethicist known for coming up with thought experiments such as his teletransportation paradox, which challenges some of our common assumptions about the nature of self and consciousness (his discussion can be found in his 1984 book *Reasons and Persons*). A key Parfitian dilemma is, given the option between surviving without psychological continuity and connectedness (Relation-R) and dying but preserving Relation-R through someone else's future existence, which is preferable? Parfit argues the latter is preferable (Fearn).

As Read explains it, Parfit's concept of this "branch-line case" hinges on teletransportation (129). Parfit imagines an individual transported to Mars; the catch is that a duplica will remain on Earth (knowing he will soon die). In the scenario that Parfit envisions, the two become separate beings (they each have their own body), but they retain the same core set of memories:

> Think of the underlying railway metaphor here: a branch line goes away from the main line and does not return to it, does not cross it again. Easily replicated if one "me" is on Mars and the other on earth. But what if we are both in the same room, after the teletransporter has done its job? What if the branch line and the main line instantly cross paths again in this way? The film version of *The Prestige* is interested in this question [Read 130].

While in Parfit's hypothetical situation, the two versions will never cross paths, the one who is soon to die is supposedly comforted by the knowledge that another version of himself will live on. As Read summarizes it, "Parfit, notoriously, goes on to argue that the 'branch-line' version of me, the 'I' in the story, shouldn't/needn't be sad that he is going to die, because he is going to survive—or at least, something is going to happen which is just as good as his surviving" (129).

The Prestige makes manifest this dilemma through the character of Robert Angier and the many clones he creates. Angier, rather than confront another version of himself and live a side-by-side existence, chooses, instead, to kill "his other self each time the teletransporter fires off. The first time, by pistol; every successive time, by having the version of himself that remains untransformed fall through a trapdoor under the stage and drown" (Read 131). Thus, *The Prestige* represents a "branch-line case with a vengeance" (Read 131). Indeed, the clones that Angier creates and then kills speak to the horror of duplication. They illustrate the monstrous consequences of technology run amuck. Not only does this technology cost the many clones their lives, but there is a heavy toll that the surviving version of Angier pays, as well. As Read notes, "the series of murders takes a terrible psychical toll on Angier" (136).

Indeed, Angier pays such a high cost for mastering the "Transported Man" trick that it leaves one to wonder, if his only goal was to perfect this illusion, then why did he not just clone himself once and then use the clone as part of his act night after night? One possibility is that Angier is, in fact, quite deliberately punishing himself for wife's death. A scene which occurs early in the film supports this interpretation. Well before he has acquired the machine which allows him to duplicate himself, there is a scene where the camera pans in on Angier placing his face in a sink to simulate drowning. As he holds his face under water, he thinks of his wife and her horrific death by drowning onstage (which the film represents by showing the image of her dying flashing by). By sending a version of himself to the tank to drown, he is symbolically connecting to his wife's death since she also died in a water tank.

Another theory is that Angier is so horror-struck by the existence of his doppelganger that he sees no choice other than to kill him. Clones have long-been associated with the uncanny and seen as a source of horror, so it would not be surprising if the thought of not only confronting but co-existing with his clone is too much for Angier too bear. As William Ian Miller underscores, "doubling disconcerts us" and "duplication is uncanny" to the human imagination (81; 82). Beyond this, he argues that, as a society, "cloning appalls us, unnerves us, disgusts, horrifies, and revolts us, precisely because it engages our deepest concerns about person-hood" (81). As Miller's comments highlight, cloning produces anxiety precisely because it challenges how we see ourselves.

Indeed, according to Michael J. Klein, who discusses clones and other forms of doubles in his essay "Beholding the Uncanny: Replicants, Cyborgs, and Clones in Science Fiction," the creation of artificial life forms such as clones has long been a source of tension, particularly for the way beings such as clones trouble boundaries. As he emphasizes, "blurring the clean division between natural and artificial life forces the characters, and the audience, to re-examine their own definitions of what it means to be human" (Klein 141). These anxieties get reflected not only in the manner the audience views Angier, but also in the way that he ends up seeing himself. As Read emphasizes, while Borden's double is "his twin, his 'other half,'" Angier's double "appears to him as a threat, a rival personage" (139).

One issue that the film leaves up for debate is whether Angier always possessed the murderous spirit that he exhibits late in the film, or if his monstrous tendencies are the result of so much duplication. Indeed, by the film's end, Angier has clearly transformed into a monstrous murderer. Not only does Angier create and then kill countless versions of himself, recall that "Angier is also effectively the murderer of one of the Borden twins. He frames Borden for his own murder by arranging for Borden to be discovered outside the water tank containing his drowned double and by not reappearing himself during the show when Borden goes below stage to examine the illusion" (McGowan 29). Even when Borden is in police custody, Angier continues torment him. Not content to leave well enough alone, Angier goes as far as to taunt Borden by visiting him in prison. He also arranges it so that he will gain custody of Borden's young daughter—much to Borden's chagrin.

To be sure, beyond the toll the rivalry takes on the men, there is a high cost to others, as well. As Claire Molloy notes in her article "Christopher Nolan and Indie Sensibilities," both "suicide and the violent death of women feature in *The Prestige* where Sarah, Borden's wife, hangs herself, and Julia, Angier's wife, drowns during an illusion, on stage in front of an audience. In the case of Angier's wife, it is revealed at the end of the film that her death was agonizing" (44).

Yet, in these cases, the role played by Angier and Borden "in each of the women's deaths remains unclear" (Molloy 44). With respect to Julia's drowning, Borden claims that he cannot remember whether he tied Angier's wife's wrists with a knot that she was unable to undo while under water. In the case of Sarah, her "suicide is blamed on her inability to come to terms with the relationship she is having, unknowingly, with both Borden and his twin, each of whom spend time with her, acting as her 'husband'" (Molloy 44).

"The brink of new terrifying possibilities"

In one of the film's final moments, Robert Angier says that the world is on "the brink of new terrifying possibilities." His remarks resonate because they hearken back to his personal experiences with technology while also suggesting more widespread technological changes on the horizon—and their potentially devastating effects. Indeed, a fact that Cojocaru calls attention to is that the film's final scenes are "set at the eve of World War I" and, in this manner, *The Prestige* thus "foreshadows the mechanized horrors to come." Since the film's action takes place during the late 19th and early 20th centuries, there is little doubt that *The Prestige* is quite consciously reflecting the anxieties common to that time period, one of which being the fear of new technologies and the havoc these new machines will wreak.

However, the film is nonetheless very much a product of the 21st century and it thus also echoes contemporary anxieties including present-day tensions related to doubling and emerging 21st century technologies. To be sure, in the 21st century, we are witnessing a new scientific revolution. Moreover, a reality of life in the 21st century is that technology is determinative of human experience—or, as Steven T. Katz puts it in his essay "Technology and Genocide: Technology as a 'Form of Life,'" in our contemporary era, "technology is a determinative, metaphysical factor" (262). Indeed, in its broader sense, technology functions "as a fundamental transformative category or modern life" (Katz 264). The transformative nature of technology is the source of much promise in contemporary life, yet it also produces anxiety. This anxiety gets reflected in *The Prestige* by the way the film depicts Angier being not only fundamentally changed but also ultimately destroyed by the same technology that has empowered him. The closing scene of the film points to this theme.

At the end of the film, it is finally revealed that "Angier has preserved his illusion by murdering himself every night, and Borden has lived his entire life as twins switching places," so that even his wife and daughter are deceived (Labuza). Indeed, as the film's final scenes make clear, "this is a secret he's willing to preserve to his death" (Labuza 41). After Borden's execution, his brother exacts revenge by shooting Angier and setting fire to his theatre. In his dying moments, Angier finally discloses his secret to Borden: "It took courage to climb into that machine every night not knowing if I'd be the man in the box or in the prestige. Do you want to see what it cost me? You didn't see where you are, did you—look ... [pointing at a long row of water tanks, now all enveloped by flames]." The camera then pans to the countless water tanks filled with the corpses of Angier's many doubles: "each tank is a coffin, the basement of Angier's theatre a graveyard of suicides" (Heilmann 25).

This final scene is rich with symbolism. For one, it connects symbolically with the death of Angier's wife Julia, since she died by drowning in a water tank. The image also brings to mind amniotic fluid and thus suggests a connection between reproduction and technology—and the anxieties that this combination produces. To be sure, the water tanks suggest both a womb and a tomb, thereby further underscoring the point that technology has the power to both create and destroy, a theme which has persisted throughout the film. Moreover, the image of the tanks function as a source of horror, since they lay bare the means by which Angier has been performing his illusion. They showcase in vivid form how the technology he has relied upon has gone beyond nature by duplicating Angier in an unnatural way. They also reveal the devastating consequences of duplication taken to the extreme and technology run amuck. As this final scene makes clear, the film's treatment of the doppelganger theme highlights the fear associated with becoming multiple while also addressing anxieties related to emerging technologies.

Indeed, in this scene and in many others, *The Prestige* demonstrates the versatility of the figure of the doppelganger. The film also calls attention to how the double can operate as a cultural vehicle to bring to the forefront the concerns of a given era. In the case of Borden, the film offers an update on the twin formula and raises questions about self and identity. The case of Angier and the existence of his many clones showcases the degree to which humans are evolving with technology and highlights the many cultural anxieties which technological change brings about.

Conclusion: Cultural Anxieties and Doppelgangers in the 21st Century

"Someone once told me the definition of Hell: The last day you have on earth, the person you became will meet the person you could have become."—Anonymous

This anonymous saying strikes at the heart of a contemporary fear: the fear of self. In fact, this quotation, which lends itself to multiple interpretations, suggests the *many* reasons we have to fear ourselves. We have cause to fear our darker impulses to be sure, but we also might feel held hostage at the prospect of being compared to the best possible versions of ourselves. Indeed, while many of us are haunted by our failures and feel threatened by our potential to fall short, we are also troubled by the thought of what we might have become, had we taken chances instead of letting opportunities pass us by. Indeed, for many of us, the mistakes we have made and the chances we did not take might haunt us in equal measure. Alongside these fears linger thoughts about the possible paths we might have taken which could have led to other possible lives. Such is the source of much anxiety. These anxieties have long existed and indeed, even into the 21st century, concerns about identity persist and are widespread—and they often lead to difficult questions about autonomy, free will, and choice.

Since potential possible paths can be illustrated so vividly and compellingly through the literary device of doubling, fictional representations of doppelgangers are now commonplace—and they are often relied upon to bring important identity-related questions to bear. As Amit Marcus highlights: "Double narratives and clone narratives highlight existential questions that science and rational thought cannot satisfactorily answer: what constitutes individuality? Is the human subject unified or split? What are the mental, social, and cultural processes that destabilize and dissolve the subject, and how do they function?" (370). Indeed, because these are cultural concerns, these subjects frequently get explored in the storylines of creative works like novels, television shows, or films.

Contemporary Narratives of Doubling: In Literature and on the Screen

Indeed, popular culture portrayals of doppelgangers have never been as common as they are today. Without a doubt, there are a good many examples of doppelgangers in contemporary narratives. These include the numerous representations of twins, ghostly doubles, mechanical doppelgangers, allohistorical doppelgangers, clones, and other forms of look-a-likes that emerge in fiction, television, and film. The fact that contemporary popular culture is brimming with examples of the figure illustrates the degree to which the doppelganger remains both a timely and enduring image. What is it that accounts for the durability of the figure? Why do various forms of doubles continue to reemerge in popular narratives?

As Marcus notes, "both double narratives and clone narratives challenge the Western conception of a separate and coherent self and the derived conceptions of moral agency and moral responsibility" (389). The figure thus remains important for the way it challenges ideas about the self and identity, notions which are being redefined in the current era. Fictional works not only call attention to these issues, but they also open up spaces for these models to be re-examined.

Narratives about doubling share much in common, but there nonetheless remains important facets which distinguish them. While some narratives—oftentimes both deliberately and self-consciously—play on and revise older formulas as part of their modes of storytelling, other texts are notable for the way they break new ground in terms of their representations. The effect is that texts use the trope of the doppelganger to, alternately, revisit timeless concerns and bring to the forefront contemporary questions. This practice highlights both the durability and malleability of the perennial figure. It also underscores how the doppelganger can function as a cultural vehicle, and thus change in response to shifting cultural norms and emerging technologies. A more detailed discussion of these trends in fictional representations of doubling will illustrate these qualities.

Revising Traditional Formulas in 21st Storylines

Certain of the narratives discussed in this book engage with questions related to identity by reworking traditional formulas. While texts about doubling clearly rely upon older formulas, many latter day narratives also push the boundaries in the way they engage with debates which have taken new form in contemporary times. For instance, while Audrey Niffenegger's *Her Fearful Symmetry* was published in 2009, its plot centers on a family melodrama and, as a whole, the novel recalls the gothic tradition, even to the point that it contains a ghost story. Its treatment of the concept of twinning hearkens back to older depictions of doubles that were popular in previous eras. Yet, the novel also quite self-consciously brings to mind 21st century debates about identity and provokes contemporary cultural anxieties related to multiplicity.

Similarly, although José Saramago's *The Double* (2002) is a 21st century text, it undoubtedly borrows from older literary traditions in the way it depicts the figure of the doppelganger. To be sure, this novel echoes well-known literary works like Poe's story "William Wilson," and Dostoevsky's novella *The Double*. Nonetheless, in this novel Saramago also makes obvious reference to the role of technology by the way he relies on a VCR and various video recorded copies of movies as important plot devices. In this regard, Saramago represents the doppelganger in a way that ties contemporary concerns (such as the anxieties that technology produces) with long-standing questions about self-hood.

Along the same lines, the television dramas *Ringer* (2011–2012) and *The Lying Game* (2011–2013) rely on the good twin/bad twin formula that was popular in the 20th century—and they thus hearken back to dramatic patterns made popular in previous eras—but also engage with recent controversies by referencing the types of scandals that became popular internet fodder in the first decade of the 21st century. For example, *Ringer* includes storylines which revolve around Ponzi schemes, organized crime, and the war on drugs, while *The Lying Game* depicts high dollar medical malpractice suits as well as storylines about the still relatively recent real estate crisis.

Narratives about Clones and the Perils of Progress

In addition to the existence of narratives which play with, but ultimately revise, older patterns, in the 21st century there also emerged a rash of storylines which constitute a new formula. Clone narratives, stories which address human cloning, became a popular subject in the aftermath of the successful cloning of Dolly, the sheep, in 1996. These storylines raise ethical questions about the practice of human cloning while also bringing concerns related to identity and self-hood to the forefront. In this manner, many of these texts also bring up ethical questions pertaining to the limits of biotechnology, while simultaneously troubling traditional conceptions of individualism and the self.

Novels such as Ishiguro's *Never Let Me Go* (2002) and Lafferty's *Six Wakes* (2017) imagine societies where human cloning has become commonplace. They thus reflect on the practice and its attendant concerns. At the same time, these novels also call into question traditional definitions of both the self and the human. In much the same way, BBC America's television series *Orphan Black* (2013–2017) pushes boundaries with its representations of the Project Leda clones, a group of female clones whose ontological and legal status remain very much up for debate. Moreover, especially in its early seasons, *Orphan Black* places a focus on questions related to self-awareness since it is only through a process of discovery that the Project Leda clones learn about—and come to terms with—the fact that they are clones and the result of human experimentation.

Similarly, the big-budget films *The Island* (2005), directed by Michael Bay, and *Oblivion* (2013), directed by Joseph Kosinski, center on cloned beings who are, at first, unaware of their true nature. In these narratives, they only later realize that they have been created for unscrupulous purposes. Like in *Orphan Black*, in both of these films, the process of clones coming to terms with the reality of their existence works to forward the action and, eventually, bring about resolution to their respective plots. Like many storylines that involve clones, these narratives question the ethics of human cloning while also provoking cultural anxieties of the current era, especially those related to the perils of (so-called) progress.

Allohistorical Doppelgangers in/and the Multiverse

Another trope which remains quite popular into the 21st century concerns the multiverse theory. Indeed, in several recent science fiction texts, the plot formula of parallel universes appears side-by-side with representations of doppelgangers. Allohistorical doppelgangers thus result from narratives which use plot devices such as time travel or parallel universes—and, indeed, science fiction texts frequently rely upon interdimensional travel to explain the existence of doubles.

The television show *Fringe* (2008–2013), for example, uses the motif of doubling, which is justified in the series by the existence of parallel universes (certain of the show's characters can travel between these dimensions), to illustrate the degree experiences shape us. *Fringe* thus underscores the fact that identity is fluid, rather than remaining stable and fixed. Similarly, the recent novels *Dark Matter* (2016) by Blake Crouch, and *Version Control* (2016) by Dexter Palmer, feature these trends since their storylines use the trope of parallel universes to discuss identity and to explore their protagonists' different possible lives. All of these texts also reflect the widespread cultural ambivalence about technology that defines our era.

Mechanical Doppelgangers?
Battlestar Galactica and *Westworld*

Another type of doppelganger makes an appearance in two 21st century cable television series, *Battlestar Galactica* (2004–2009) and *Westworld* (2016–present). While a form of the mechanical doppelganger appears in both of these series, these narratives offer a fresh update on the traditional trope. Indeed, while both series rely on traditional representations of robotic counterparts, they ultimately push the boundaries through their portrayals of doubling.

In the case of *Battlestar Galactica*, which is a 21st century reimagining of a television show from the 1970s, the Cylons are both cyborgs (who are able to easily "pass" as humans) and doppelgangers; as beings, they thus complicate ontological questions by calling into question—and ultimately dissolving—binaries such as human/machine, thinking/programming, and natural/artificial. *Westworld* is also a re-imagined product. The contemporary series offer an update of a movie from 1973 and, like *Battlestar Galactica*, presents a 21st century version of the mechanical doppelganger through the character of Bernard Lowe (a sentient AI), who is an exact replica of man named Arnold Weber. Bernard proves to be an interesting case in point, not least of all because he, for a number of episodes, remains unaware of both the fact that he is an AI and a copy of another person.

Monstrous Multiplicity in *The Prestige*

The Prestige (2005), a film directed by Christopher Nolan, actually offers competing visions of doubling by representing characters who bring different types of doppelgangers into debate. Indeed, the film relies upon both twins and clones as part of its plot, which centers on rival magicians who vie for stage success. Alfred Borden, one of these men, pulls off a magnificent stage illusion because he is actually two men: twin brothers who share the same life. The other man, Robert Angier, performs an unbelievable stage feat because he has access to a duplicating machine which he uses to make clones of himself.

With respect to Borden and Angier alike, it is worth pointing out that both veer into the realm of the monstrous due to the way they test the boundaries between human and other. Moreover, they also prove monstrous by what they are willing to do—and because of the many anxieties their existence provokes. In this manner, the film relies on the motif of doubling to caution against too much progress and to reflect anxieties related to technology and new breakthroughs.

To be sure, *The Prestige*, like so many of the other narratives about doubling that are examined in this book, showcases the versatility of the figure of the doppelganger. Like these many other texts, Nolan's film also calls attention to how the double can operate as a cultural vehicle to bring to the forefront the concerns of a given era. Indeed, at its core, this is the power of the figure, and the reason why it not only persists, but remains both popular and prevalent even into the 21st century.

Doubling on the Horizon: Emerging Texts and Emerging Technologies

While the many cases of fictional doubling addressed in this book are meant to be representative, they are by no means exhaustive. The popularity and pervasiveness of representations of multiplicity in contemporary fiction, television, and film make it difficult to discuss every storyline involving doubles. Indeed, even as this book is being written, there are still more cultural texts emerging that rely on the figure of the doppelganger—and these examples from popular culture reflect many of the same anxieties related to technology that can frequently be found in the contemporary representations discussed in this book's preceding chapters.

Take, for instance, the very recent case of the re-imagined *Twin Peaks* television series, which is a remake of the short-lived but cultishly popular series created by Mark Frost and David Lynch, which aired on ABC in the early 1990s (it is worth pointing out that David Lynch is well-known for "doubling"). The original series, *Twin Peaks* (1990–1991), and its prequel, a movie entitled *Twin Peaks: Fire Walk with Me* (1992), concerned the murder of Laura Palmer, the local Homecoming Queen, and the ensuing investigation (her body was found washed up on a riverbank in the first episode of the series, prompting FBI involvement in the case). Notably, many of the episodes contain treatment of the theme of doubling, including through the rather conspicuous presence of the doppelgangers of dead people that would frequently appear in episodes of the series.

The 21st century update of the series, *Twin Peaks: The Return* (2017), a Showtime Original series, was also created by Mark Frost and David Lynch. It represents a continuation of the original series and focuses on some of the same characters including FBI Special Agent Dale Cooper (played by original star Kyle MacLachlan, who also plays the role of Cooper's doppelganger), but it also brings to bear concerns related to technology and its role. Specifically, the 2017 series, albeit implicitly and vis-à-vis a dream sequence, raises questions about the degree to which scientific progress should be governed by ethics. This subject emerges in the eighth episode, which presents as a curious window into the 20th century by featuring a surreal plot which concerns an early detonation of an atomic bomb and its horrifying (and bizarre) consequences. Writing for *The New York Times*, Noel Murray describes the episode as follows: "Not even the jarring nightmare sequences from the original series were anything like this hour, which jumps around in time and space in ways that at times seem almost like free association. An extended stretch of this week's episode takes place in the wake of a 1945 atomic bomb test in White Sands, N.M., and thrusts the audience deep into the physical, emotional and metaphorical space of a mushroom cloud." Though some viewers have suggested that "Part 8" might be best understood as a stand-alone episode, Brian Tallerico, instead, recommends that viewers should "think of 'Part 8' as a mirror reflecting the themes of the series." Indeed, using the lens that Tallerico proposes, the series calls into question the consequences of technology run amuck by metaphorically (and surrealistically) representing the destructive capabilities of 20th century technology. The episode, particularly by the way it emphasizes the passing of time, seems to be suggesting if 20th century technology has such destructive power, then what fresh horrors might this new century bring?

Undeniably, new technologies are emerging in the 21st century at a never before seen rate. These advancements have the potential to better human lives, but they also could have dire consequences. Hence, as a result, there is friction between the promise and problems associated with these developments, and cultural anxieties take hold. These anxieties are the product of widespread cultural ambivalence related to 21st century technologies. They also are the result of the ambivalence we feel about our increasingly fractured notion of identity, a concept which has been ushered in by—and proves symptomatic of—the postmodern era.

To be sure, doppelgangers have never been more prevalent in popular culture than they are today. Jen Chaney emphasizes this sentiment in "Why Are There So Many Doppelgängers in Pop Culture Right Now?" In this recent article, Chaney addresses the pervasiveness of doppelgangers, noting that "the worlds of film and television are currently riddled with doppelgängers." Moreover, according to Chaney, their pervasiveness is "purposeful." As she sums it up, "at the present moment, it makes sense to assume a twin might make an appearance in anything you might be watching" (Chaney).

Indeed, as new technologies emerge, so, too, do new texts that call into question the kind of impacts that they may one day have on all of us. The new texts so frequently employ the literary motif of the doppelganger. As this continuing trend suggests, the popularity of the figure is not waning. Instead, it remains pervasive and thus worthy of examination.

Bibliography

Anolik Bienstock, Ruth, and Howard, Douglas L., eds. *The Gothic Other: Racial and Social Constructions in the Literary Imagination*. McFarland, 2004. Print.

Atwood, Margaret. "Brave New World: Kazuo Ishiguro's Novel Really Is Chilling." *Slate Magazine*, 1 April 2005. Web. Accessed 22 May 2017.

Bailly, Christian. *Automata: The Golden Age 1848–1914*. Robert Hale Publishers, 2003. Print.

Banks, Carolyn. "Double Trouble." *The Washington Post*, 1 August 1993. Web. Accessed 21 June 2017.

Banville, John. "*The Double*: The Tears of a Clone." *The New York Times*, 10 October 2004. Web. Accessed 18 May 2017.

Battis, Jes. *Investigating Farscape: Uncharted Territories of Sex and Science Fiction*. I.B. Tauris, 2007. Print.

Baudrillard, Jean. *Screened Out*. Verso, 2002. Print.

Bedford, Robert H. "Clones in a Locked Room Murder Mystery in Spaaaaace! *Six Wakes* by Mur Lafferty." *Tor: Book Reviews*, 31 January 2017. Web. Accessed 20 June 2017.

Bennett, Betty T. *The Letters of Mary Wollstonecraft Shelley, Volume 1*. Johns Hopkins University Press, 1980. Print.

Bignell, Jonathan. *Media Semiotics: An Introduction, Second Edition*. Manchester University Press, 2002. Print.

_____. "Seeing and Knowing: Reflexivity and Quality." *Quality TV: Contemporary American Television and Beyond*. Edited by Janet McCabe and Kim Akass. I.B Tauris, 2007. pp. 158–170. Print.

Blum, Joanne. *Transcending Gender: The Male/Female Double in Women's Fiction*. UMI Research Press, 1988. Print.

Booth, Paul. *Playing Fandom: Negotiating Fandom and Media in the Digital Age*. University of Iowa Press, 2015. Print.

Brake, Mark, and Hook, Neil. *Different Engines: How Science Drives Fiction and Fiction Drives Science*. Macmillan, 2008. Print.

Brooker, Will. "Are You Watching Closely?" *The Cinema of Christopher Nolan: Imagining the Impossible*. Edited by Jacqueline Furby and Stuart Joy. Columbia University Press, 2015. Print. pp. xi-xiii.

Brooks, Peter. "Storytelling without Fear? Confession in Law and Literature." *Law's Stories: Narrative and Rhetoric in the Law*. Edited by Peter Brooks and Paul Gewirtz. Yale University Press, 1996. pp. 114–34. Print.

Burrows, David J., and Shawcross, John T., eds. *Myths and Motifs in Literature*. Free Press, 1973. Print.

Butler, Marilyn. "The Woman at the Window: Ann Radcliffe in the Novels of Mary Wollstonecraft and Jane Austen." *Gender and Literary Voice*. Edited by Janet Todd. Holmes and Meier, 1980, Print.

Caplan, Art. *Smart Mice, Not-So-Smart People: An Interesting and Amusing Guide to Bioethics*. Rowman & Littlefield, 2007. Print.

Carroll, Rachel. "Imitations of Life: Cloning, Heterosexuality, and the Human in Kazuo Ishiguro's *Never Let Me Go*."

Journal of Gender Studies, Volume 19, Issue 1 (March 2010): pp. 59–71. Print.

Chaney, Jen. "Why Are There So Many Doppelgängers in Pop Culture Right Now?" *Vulture*, 2 June 2017. Web. Accessed 11 June 2017.

Cobb, Gerald T. "A Dilemma of Identity." *American Magazine*, 11 October 2004. Web. Accessed 23 May 2017.

Cojocaru, Daniel. "Man's Desire Exceeds His Grasp—*The Prestige* as Utopia." *Journal of Religion & Film*, Volume 14, Issue 1 (2016). Web.

Colebrook, Claire. "Time That Is Intolerant." *Memory in the Twenty-First Century: New Critical Perspectives from the Arts, Humanities, and Sciences.* Edited by Sebastian Groes. Springer, 2016: pp. 147–158. Print.

Conrad, Joseph. "The Secret Sharer" (1909). *Heart of Darkness and The Secret Sharer*. Introduction by Joyce Carol Oates. Signet Classic, 1997. Print.

Dahlstrom, Linda. "Just Because We Can Do Something, Should We? Art Caplan Weighs in on the Latest Controversies in His New Book." *Breaking Bioethics on NBC News*. 10 November 2006. Web. Accessed 29 May 2017.

Daniels, Tony. "*PW* Talks with Blake Crouch: Alternate Worlds, Alternate Selves." *Publishers Weekly*, 16 May 2016. pp. 34. Print.

Dasen, V. "Multiple Births in Ancient Medical Texts." *Gesnerus*, Volume 55 (1998): pp. 183–204. Print.

Davidson, H.R. Ellis. *Gods and Myths of Northern Europe*. Penguin, 1965. Print.

De Camp, L. Sprague. *Lest Darkness Fall* (1939). Ballantine Books, 1983. Print.

de Nooy, Juliana. *Twins in Contemporary Literature and Culture: Look Twice*. Palgrave, 2005. Print.

de Sousa Caetano, Joana Catarina. "Memories are Forever: Transhumanism and Cultural Memory in *V for Vendetta*, *Oblivion*, and *The Giver*." *Via Panorâmica*, Volume 3, Number 5 (2016): pp. 29–38.

Derry, Charles. *The Suspense Thriller: Films in the Shadow of Alfred Hitchcock*. McFarland, 1988. Print.

Dewar, Elaine. *The Second Tree: Of Clones, Chimeras and Quests for Immortality*. Vintage, 2010. Web.

Deutsch, David. *The Beginning of Infinity: Explanations that Transform the World*. Penguin, 2013. Web.

D'Hoker, Elke. "Confession and Atonement in Contemporary Fiction: J. M. Coetzee, John Banville, and Ian McEwan." *Critique: Studies in Contemporary Fiction* Volume 48, Number 1 (2006): pp. 31–43. Print.

Dietz, Frank. "Secret Sharers: The Doppelgänger Motif in Speculative Fiction." *The Fantastic Other: An Interface of Perspectives*. Edited by Brett Cooke, George E. Slusser, and Jaime Marti-Olivella. Rodopi, 1998. pp. 209–220. Print.

Dickens, Charles. *A Tale of Two Cities* (1859). Edited by Simon Schama. Vintage Books, 1990. Print.

Doctorow, Cory. "I've Created a Monster! And So Can You." *Slate*, 29 May 2017. Web. Accessed 30 May 2017.

Dostoevsky, Fyodor. *The Double* (1846). Dover Publications. 1997. Print.

Eberstadt, Fernanda. "José Saramago, Nobel Prize-Winning Portuguese Writer, Dies at 87." *The New York Times*, 18 June 2010. Web. Accessed 11 May 2017.

Eddington, Arthur Stanley. *Space, Time, and Gravitation: An Outline of the General Relativity Theory*. Cambridge University Press, 1920. Print.

Elias, Norbert. *The Established and the Outsiders*. Sage, 1994. Print.

Eminem and Rihanna. "The Monster." *The Marshall Mathers LP2*, Aftermath/Shady/Interscope, 2013. Web.

Engel, William E. *Early Modern Poetics in Melville and Poe: Memory, Melancholy, and the Emblematic Tradition*. Ashgate, 2012. Print.

"The Ethics of Cloning to Produce Children." *President's Council on Bioethics: Human Cloning and Human Dignity: An Ethical Inquiry—Full Report*. 2002. Web. Accessed 26 May 2017.

Fearn, Nicholas. *The Latest Answers to the Oldest Questions: a Philosophical Adventure with the World's Greatest Thinkers*. Grove Press, 2005. Print.

Fernbach, Amanda. *Fantasies of Fetishism: From Decadence to the Post Human*. Edinburgh University Press, 2002. Print.

Ferreira, Maria Aline Salgueiro Seabra. *I am the Other: Literary Negotiations of Human Cloning.* Praeger, 2005. Print.

Flood, Alison. "*Dark Matter* Review: Quantum Fiction that's Delightfully Unserious." *The Guardian*, 22 August 2016. Web. Accessed 11 June 2017.

Fonseca, Tony. "The Doppelgänger." *Icons of Horror and the Supernatural: An Encyclopedia of Our Worst Nightmares*, Volume 1. Edited by S.T. Joshi. Greenwood, 2007. pp. 187–193. Print.

Frazer, James George. *The Golden Bough Part I: The Magic Art and the Evolution of Kings, Volume 1.* Macmillan, 1922. Print.

Fringe. Created by J. J. Abrams, Alex Kurtzman, and Roberto Orc. Bad Robot and Warner Brothers, 2008–2013. DVD.

Garofalo, Daisy. "Shakespeare's Twins." *Wellcome Library*. 2016. Web. Accessed 11 April 2017. http://blog.wellcomelibrary.org/2016/04/shakespeares-twins/.

Gaskell, Elizabeth Cleghorn. *The Poor Clare* (1856). Melville House Publishing, 2013. Print.

George, Susan A. "Investigating the Postmodern Memory Crisis on the Small Screen." *Practicing Science Fiction: Critical Essays on Writing, Reading and Teaching*. Edited by Karen Hellekson, Craig B. Jacobsen, Patrick B. Sharp, and Lisa Yaszek. McFarland, 2010. Print. pp. 104–116.

Geraghty, Lincoln. *American Science Fiction Film and Television*. Berg Press, 2009. Print.

Gergen, Kenneth. *The Saturated Self: Dilemmas of Identity in Contemporary Life*. New York: Basic Books, 1991. Print.

Gerrick, Christopher Joseph. *Fear of the In-Between: Interstitial Space in Edgar Allan Poe's "William Wilson."* Master's Thesis. Rice University, 2003. Web. Accessed 11 May 2017.

Gleick, James. *Time Travel: A History*. Pantheon, 2016. Print.

Goodman, Tim. "*Orphan Black*: TV Review." *The Hollywood Reporter*, 15 April 2014. Web. Accessed 11 April 2017.

Graham, Elaine L. *Representations of the Post/Human: Monsters, Aliens, and Others in Popular Culture*. Rutgers University Press, 2002. Print.

Grainge, Paul. *Monochrome Memories: Nostalgia and Style in Retro America*. Prager, 2002. Print.

Griffin, Gabriele. "Science and the Cultural Imaginary: The Case of Kazuo Ishiguro's *Never Let Me Go*." *Textual Practice*, Volume 23 (2009): pp. 645–663. Print.

Grubbs, Jefferson. "Is Bernard Arnold On *Westworld*? It's More Complicated Than That." *Bustle*, 27 November 2016. Web. Accessed 27 June 2017.

Guenther, Corey L., and Alick, Mark D. "Psychology of the Self." *Oxford Bibliographies: Psychology*. Oxford University Press. 18 May 2017. Web. Accessed 26 May 2017.

Haas, Elizabeth, et al. *Projecting Politics Political Messages in American Films*. Taylor and Francis, 2015. Print.

Hanafi, Zakiya. *The Monster in the Machine: Magic, Medicine, and the Marvelous in the Time of the Scientific Revolution*. Duke University Press, 2000. Web.

Haraway, Donna. *Simians, Cyborgs, and Women*. Routledge, 1991. Print.

Harrod, Mary Beth. *Making Confessions: The Confessional Voice Found Among Literary Genres*. Thesis. SUNY Brockport, 2007. Print.

Harvey, David. *The Condition of Postmodernity: An Enquiry into the Origins of Cultural Change*. Blackwell, 1990. Print.

Hayles, N. Katherine. *How We Became Post-Human: Virtual Bodies in Cybernetics, Literature, and Informatics*. University of Chicago Press, 1999. Print.

Heilmann, Ann. "Doing It with Mirrors: Neo-Victorian Metatextual Magic in *Affinity*, *The Prestige*, and *The Illusionist*." *Neo-Victorian Studies* 2.2 (2009): 2009–2010. Print.

Heller, Jason. "*Six Wakes* is a Nerve-Tingling Interstellar Murder Mystery." *NPR: Books*, 31 January 2017. Web. Accessed. 20 June, 2017.

_____. "*Version Control* is a Dizzying Elevation of The Time-Travel Tale." *NPR: Books*, 26 February 2016. Web. Accessed 11 June 11, 2017.

Hill, Rebecca A. "In the Box Lies Dark Matter: An Interview with Blake Crouch." *Voice of Youth Advocates*, Volume 39,

Number 5 (December 2016). pp. 40–41. Print.

Hills, Matt. *Fan Culture*. Routledge, 2002. Print.

Hoben, John. "Reading Alien Suns: Using SF Fiction to Teach a Political Literacy of Possibility." *Science Fiction and Speculative Fiction: Challenging Genres*. Edited by P.L. Thomas. Sense Publishers, 2013. pp. 95–118. Print.

Holliday, Christopher. "Elysium." *Science Fiction Film and Television*, Volume 7, Number 3 (2014): pp. 433–434. Print.

Hood, Bruce M. *The Self Illusion: Why There is No 'You' Inside Your Head*. Little, Brown, and Company. 2012. Print.

Horn, John. "You Call this Paradise? Cloning Takes a Haunting Turn in *The Island*, the Latest Action Fare from Director Michael Bay, Who's Had a Few Nightmares of His Own." *LA Times*, 17 July 2005: E5. Print.

Huet, Marie Hélène. *Monstrous Imagination*. Harvard University Press, 1993. Print.

Hühn, Peter. "The Detective as Reader: Narrativity and Reading Concepts in Detective Fiction." *Modern Fiction Studies* Volume 3, Number 3 (1987): pp. 451–466. Print.

Ingebretsen, Edward J. "Staking the Monster: A Politics of Remonstrance." *Religion and American Culture: A Journal of Interpretation*, Volume 8, Number 1 (1999): pp. 91–116. Print.

Ishiguro, Kazuo. *Never Let Me Go*. Faber & Faber, 2005. Print.

The Island. Dir. Michael Bay. Perf. Scarlett Johansson, Ewan McGregor, Djimon Hounsou. Warner Brothers 2005. DVD.

Jafari, Morteza. "Freud's Uncanny: The Role of the Double in *Jane Eyre* and *Wuthering Heights*." *Victorian Newsletter*, Issue 118 (Fall 2010): pp. 43–53. Print.

James, Henry. "The Jolly Corner" (1908). *Complete Stories, 1898–1910*. Library of America, 1996. Print.

Jancovich, Mark, and Lyons, James, eds. *Quality Popular Television: Cult TV, the Industry and Fans*. British Film Institute, 2003. Print.

Jerng, Mark. "Giving Form to Life: Cloning and Narrative Expectations of the Human." *Partial Answers: Journal of Literature and the History of Ideas*, Volume 6 Number 2 (2008): pp. 369–393. Print.

Jones, Nick. "Review of *Oblivion*." *Science Fiction Film and Television*, Volume 7, Number 2 (Summer 2014): pp. 290–294. Print.

Jones, Steve. "Cyber-punk: Cyberpunk and Information Technology." *The Journal of Popular Culture*, Volume 28, Number 2 (1994): Pp. 81–92. Print.

Jusino, Teresa. "What *Orphan Black*'s M.K. and Kira Teach Us about Female Bodily Autonomy." *The Mary Sue*, 22 June 2017. Web. Accessed 22 June 2017.

Kaplan, E.A., and Squier, S., eds. *Playing Dolly: Technocultural Formations, Fantasies, and Fictions of Assisted Reproduction*. Rutgers University Press, 1999. Print.

Katz, Steven T. "Technology and Genocide: Technology as a 'Form of Life.'" *Echoes from the Holocaust: Philosophical Reflections on a Dark Time* (1998). Edited by Alan Rosenberg. Temple University Press, 2009. 262–291. Print.

Khair, Tabish. *The Gothic, Postcolonialism and Otherness: Ghosts from Elsewhere*. Palgrave, 2009. Print.

Kirk, Terry. "Monumental Monstrosity, Monstrous Monumentally." *Perspecta*, Volume 40: Monster Special Issue (2008): pp. 6–15. Print.

Klein, Michael J. "Beholding the Uncanny: Replicants, Cyborgs and Clones in Science Fiction." *Humanity in Cybernetic Environments*. Edited by Daniel Riha. Interdisciplinary Press, 2010. Print. pp. 137–145.

Klein, Stan, and Nichols, Shaun. "Memory and the Sense of Personal Identity." *Mind*, Volume 121, Number 483(2012): pp. 677–702. Print.

Kogel, Dennis, and Schäfer, Irene. "The Doppelgänger Motif in Science Fiction Film." *Of Body Snatchers and Cyber Punks: Student Essays on American Science Fiction Film*. Universitätsverlag Göttingen Press, 2011. pp. 125–142. Print.

Kolehmainen, Sophia M. "Human Cloning: Brave New Mistake." *CRG: Council for Responsible Genetics*. 2017. Web. Accessed 25 May 2017.

Kvideland, Reimund, and Sehmsdorf, Henning K. *Scandinavian Folk Belief and Legend*. University of Minnesota Press, 1989. Print.

Labuza, Peter. "Billion Dollar Noir: Christopher Nolan and the Reconstruction of Film Noir in Hollywood." *Journal of American Studies of Turkey*, Issue 32 (2012): pp. 38–43. Print.

Lafferty, Mur. "Men Are from Aquaria, Women Are from Caprica." *So Say We All: An Unauthorized Collection of Thoughts and Opinions on Battlestar Galactica*. Edited by Richard Hatch. Smart Pop, 2006. pp. 171–180. Print.

____. *Six Wakes*. Orbit, 2017. Print.

Lamble, Ryan. "*Oblivion*: A Spoiler-Filled Exploration." *Den of Geek*, 15 April 2013. Web. Accessed 4 June 2017.

Landsberg, Alison. *Prosthetic Memory: The Transformation of American Remembrance in the Age of Mass Culture*. Columbia University Press, 2004. Print.

____. "Prosthetic Memory: *Total Recall* and *Blade Runner*." *Cyberspace/ Cyberbodies/Cyberpunk: Cultures of Technological Embodiment*. Edited by Mike Featherstone and Roger Burrows. Sage, 1995. pp. 175–189. Print.

Latour, Bruno. *An Inquiry into Modes of Existence*. Harvard University Press, 2013. Print.

____. *Reassembling the Social: An Introduction to Actor-Network-Theory*. Oxford University Press, 2005. Print.

Levy, Titus. "Human Rights Storytelling and Trauma Narrative in Kazuo Ishiguro's *Never Let Me Go*." *Journal of Human Rights*, Volume 10, Issue 1 (2011): pp. 1–16. Print.

Liptak, Andrew. "*Dark Matter* is a Blockbuster Read that Channels Michael Crichton." *The Verge*, 26 July 2016. Web. Accessed 28 May 2017.

Locke, John. "Of Identity and Diversity." *An Essay Concerning Human Understanding*. Edited by John W. Yolton. Dent, 1993. Print.

Lowry, Brian. "TV Review: *Orphan Black*, Season 3." *Variety*, 18 April 2015. Web. Accessed 11 March 2017.

Madrigal, Alexis C. "There Really Are So Many More Twins Now." *Atlantic Monthly*, 14 April 2014. Web. Accessed 11 April 2017.

The Manchurian Candidate. Dir. Jonathan Demme. Perf. Denzel Washington, Meryl Streep, and Liev Schreiber. Paramount Pictures, 2004. DVD.

Mangan, Michael. *Performing Dark Arts: A Cultural History of Conjuring*. Bristol: Intellect, 2007. Print.

Manguel, Alberto. "Twins in a Spin." *The Guardian*, 6 August 2004. Web. 18 May 2017.

Marcus, Amit. "Telling the Difference: Clones, Doubles and what's in Between." *Connotations: A Journal for Critical Debate*, Volume 21, Numbers 2–3 (2011/2012): 363–396. Print.

McCarthy, Todd. "*Oblivion*: This Postapocalyptic Thriller—Starring Tom Cruise in Fine Form—Shines Best in Quiet, Poetic Moments." *Hollywood Reporter*, Volume 419, Number 14 (April 19, 2013): pp. 108. Print.

McGowan, Todd. "The Violence of Creation in *The Prestige*." *International Journal of Žižek Studies: Žižek and Cinema*, Volume 1, Number 3 (2016): pp. 1–31 Print.

Menger, Ellen R. *Casual and Hardcore Players in HBO's Westworld (2016): The Immoral and Violent Player*. Master's Thesis. Utrecht University, 2017. Print.

Molloy, Claire. "Christopher Nolan and Indie Sensibilities." *Revue Française d'Etudes Américaines*, Volume 2 (2013): pp. 40–51. Print.

Miller, William Ian. "Sheep, Joking, Cloning, and the Uncanny." *Clones and Clones: Facts and Fantasies about Human Cloning*. Edited by Martha Craven Nussbaum and Cass R. Sunstein. Norton, 1999. Print. pp. 78–87.

Mitchell, Kaye. "Bodies that Matter: Science Fiction, Technoculture, and the Gendered Body." *Science Fiction Studies*, Volume 98, Number 33 (March 2006). Web. Accessed 23 June 2017.

Morgan, Ann. "The Power of Two: Twins in Literature, From *Twelfth Night* to *The Shining* to Tweedledum and Tweedledee ... Why Are Identical Siblings so Useful in Storytelling?" *The Guardian*, 15 February 2016. Web. Accessed 28 2017.

Mullan, John. "On First Reading Kazuo Ishiguro's *Never Let Me Go*." *Kazuo Ishiguro: Contemporary Critical Perspectives*. Edited by Sean Matthews and Sebastian Groes. Bloomsbury Publishing, 2010. pp. 104–113. Print.

Murray, Noel. "*Twin Peaks* Season 3, Episode 8: White Light White Heat." *The New York Times*, 26 June 2017. Web. 29 Accessed June 2017.

Nabokov, Vladimir. *Despair* (1934). Penguin Classics, 2010. Print.

Niffenegger, Audrey. *Her Fearful Symmetry*. Scribner's, 2009. Print.

———. *The Time Traveler's Wife*. Houghton Mifflin, 2003. Print.

Nussbaum, Emily. "The Meta-Politics of *Westworld*." *The New Yorker*, 24 October 2016. Web. Accessed 25 May 2017.

Oblivion. Dir. Joseph Kosinski. Perf. Tom Cruise and Morgan Freeman. Universal Pictures, 2013. DVD.

O'Hehir, Andrew. "A Countdown Thriller in Which the Hero Inhabits Many Alternate Universes." *The New York Times*, 27 July 2016. Web. Accessed 27 May 2017.

O'Keefe, Jack. "Which *Westworld* Humans Are Hosts? Bernard May Not Be the Only Trick up Ford's Sleeve." *Bustle*, 20 November 2016. Web. Accessed 26 June 2017.

Oliver, Kelly. *Earth and World: Philosophy after the Apollo Missions*. Columbia University Press, 2015. Print.

Once Upon a Time. Created by Edward Kitsis and Adam Horowitz. ABC Studios, 2011-present. Web.

Opam, Kwame. "*Legion* Gets the Mystery Box Formula Right Where *Westworld* Failed." *The Verge*, 28 February 2017. Web. Accessed 30 April 2017.

O'Riordan, Kate. "Human Cloning in Film: Horror, Ambivalence, Hope." *Science as Culture*, Volume17, Issue 2 (July, 2008): pp. 145–162. Print.

Orphan Black. Created by John Fawcett and Graeme Manson. Temple Street Productions, 2013–2017. Web.

Orr, Christopher. "Sympathy for the Robot." *Atlantic Monthly*, 1 October 2016. Web. Accessed 25 June 2017.

Palmer, Dexter. *Version Control*. Knopf/Doubleday, 2016. Print.

Parfit, Derek. *Reasons and Persons*. Clarendon Press, 1984. Print.

Parikka, Jussi. *What is Media Archaeology?* Polity Press, 2012. Print.

Passions. Created by James E. Reilly. Outpost Farm Production/NBC Studios, 1999–2008. Web.

Poe, Edgar Allan. "William Wilson." *Edgar Allan Poe: Poetry and Tales*. Edited by Patrick F. Quinn. Library of America, 1984. pp. 337–357. Print.

Pointon, Marcia. *Portrayal and the Search for Identity*. Reaktion Books, 2013. Print.

The Prestige. 2006. Dir. Christopher Nolan. Perf. Hugh Jackman and Christian Bale. Touchstone. DVD.

Puchner, Martin. "When We Were Clones." *Raritan: A Quarterly Review*, Volume 27, Number 4 (2008): pp. 34–49. Print.

Rank, Otto. *The Double: A Psychoanalytic Study*. Edited by Harry Tucker. University of North Carolina Press, 2011. Print.

Read, Rupert. "The Tale Parfit Tells: Analytic Metaphysics of Personal Identity vs. Wittgensteinian Film and Literature." *Philosophy and Literature*, Volume 38, Number 1 (April 2015): pp. 128–153. Print.

Richter, Jean Paul. *Siebenkäs* (1796). Tradition Classics, 2012. Print.

Robinson, Joanna. "*Westworld*: The Unsettling Ramifications of That Chilling Twist." *Vanity Fair*, 13 November 2016. Web. Accessed 21 May 2017.

Roethke, Theodore. *The Collected Poems*. Anchor Books, 1975. Print.

Rorty, Amélie Oksenberg. "A Literary Postscript: Characters, Persons, Selves, Individuals." *The Identities of Persons*. University of California Press, 1976. Pp. 301–323. Print.

Rumsey, Abby Smith. *When We Are No More: How Digital Memory Is Shaping Our Future*. Bloomsbury Publishing, 2016. Web.

Schapera, I. "Customs Relating to Twins in South Africa." *Journal of the Royal African Society*, Volume 26, Number 102 (1927): pp. 117–137. Print.

Schechtman, Marya. "Personal Identity and the Past." *Philosophy, Psychiatry, and Psychology*, Volume 12, Number 1 (March, 2005): pp. 9–22. Print.

Schmid, Astrid. *The Fear of the Other: Ap-*

proaches to English Stories of the Double (1764–1910). Peter Lang, 1996. Print.
Schwartz, Hillel. *The Culture of the Copy: Striking Likenesses, Unreasonable Facsimiles*. Zone Books, 1996. Print.
Seaman-Grant, Zoe E. *Constructing Womanhood and the Female Cyborg: A Feminist Reading of Ex Machina and Westworld*. Honors Thesis. Bates College, 2017. Print.
Sencindiver, Susan Yi. "Sexing or Specularising the Doppelgänger: A Recourse to Poe's 'Ligeia.'" *Fear Itself: Reasoning the Unreasonable*. Edited by Stephen Hessel and Michèle Huppert. Rodopi, 2010. pp. 63–86. Print.
Sexton, Anne. *Transformations* (1971). Houghton Mifflin, 2001. Print.
Shakespeare, William. *The Complete Works of Shakespeare*. Edited by David M. Bevington. Longman, 1997. Print.
Shildrick, Margrit. "Transgressing the Law with Foucault and Derrida: Some Reflections on Anomalous Embodiment." *Critical Quarterly*, Volume 47, Number 3 (2005): pp. 30–46. Print.
Sliding Doors. 1998. Dir. Peter Howitt. Perf. Gwyneth Paltrow. Miramax. DVD.
Smolenski, Phil and Elsby, Charlene. "*Fringe* and 'If Science Can Do It, Then Science Ought to Do It.'" *The Philosophy of J.J. Abrams*. Edited by Patricia Brace and Robert Arp. University Press of Kentucky, 2014. pp. 101–116. Print.
Spence, Louise. *Watching Daytime Soap Operas: The Power of Pleasure*. Wesleyan University Press, 2005. Print.
Stockly, Ed. "Saturday's TV Highlights and Weekend Talk: *Orphan Black*." *LA Times*, 17 April 2015. Web. Accessed 10 April 2017.
Suarez, J.M. "Tatiana Maslany Continues to Astound in *Orphan Black* Season Two." *Pop Matters*, 24 July 2014. Web. Accessed 11 June 2016.
Tallerico, Brian. "Our 5 Biggest Questions after *Twin Peaks: The Return*, Episode 8." *Vulture*, 26 June 2017. Web. Accessed 29 June 2017.
Tally, Robert T. *Poe and the Subversion of American Literature: Satire, Fantasy, Critique*. Bloomsbury. 2014. Print.
Taylor, Timothy. *The Artificial Ape: How Technology Changed the Course of Human Evolution*. Palgrave, 2010. Print.
Thompson, Robert J. *Television's Second Golden Age: From Hill Street Blues to ER*. Syracuse University Press, 1997. Print.
Toker, Leona, and Chertoff, Daniel. "Reader Response and the Recycling of Topoi in Kazuo Ishiguro's *Never Let Me Go*." *Partial Answers: Journal of Literature and the History of Ideas*, Volume 6, Number 1 (January 2008): pp. 163–180. Print.
Torchwood. Developed by Russel T. Davies. BBC Wales/Canadian Broadcasting Company. 2006–2011. DVD.
Totaro, Donato. "The Contemporary Doppelgänger." *Offscreen*, Volume 2, Issue 1 (January 1998). Web. Accessed 11 April 2017.
Tsao, Tiffany. "The Tyranny of Purpose: Religion and Biotechnology in Ishiguro's *Never Let Me Go*." *Literature & Theology*, Volume 26, Number 2 (June 2012): pp. 214–232. Print.
Turkle, Sherry. *Life on the Screen: Identity in the Age of the Internet*. Simon & Schuster, 1995. Print.
"20 Films about Doubles and Doppelgängers." *Indie Wire*, 13 March 2014. Web. Accessed 11 June 2017.
Twin Peaks. Created by Mark Frost and David Lynch. ABC. 1990–1991. DVD.
Twin Peaks, the Return. Created by Mark Frost and David Lynch. Showtime. 2017. Web.
Updike, John. "Two's a Crowd." *The New Yorker*, 27 September 2004. Web. 19 May 2017.
Urbanski, Heather. *The Science Fiction Reboot: Canon, Innovation and Fandom in Refashioned Franchises*. McFarland, 2013. Print.
Usher. "More." *Raymond V. Raymond*. LaFace/Jive, 2010. Web.
Vardoulakis, Dimitris. *The Doppelgänger: Literature's Philosophy*. Fordham University Press, 2010. Print.
Walpole, Horace. *The Castle of Otranto, a Gothic Story* (1764). Oxford University Press, 1996. Print.
Waugh, Charles G., and Greenberg, Martin Harry, eds. *Alternative Histories: Eleven Stories of the World As it Might

Have Been. Taylor and Francis, 1986. Print.

Wax, Murray, and Wax, Rosalie. "The Notion of Magic." *Current Anthropology,* Volume 4, Number 5 (December, 1963): pp. 495–518. Print.

Webber, Andrew J. *The Doppelgänger: Double Visions in German Literature.* Clarendon Press, 1996. Print.

Westworld. Created by Jonathan Nolan and Lisa Joy. HBO Entertainment/Warner Brothers. 2016-Present. Web.

"*Westworld*: The Official Website for the HBO Series." HBO.com/Westworld. Web. Accessed 26 June 2017.

Williams, Linda Ruth. *The Erotic Thriller in Contemporary Cinema.* Indiana University Press, 2005. Print.

Wolfreys, Julian. *Victorian Hauntings: Spectrality, Gothic, the Uncanny and Literature.* Palgrave, 2001. Print.

Yorke, John. "All Stories Are the Same: From *Avatar* to *The Wizard of Oz,* Aristotle to Shakespeare." *Atlantic Monthly,* 1 January 2016. Web. Accessed 21 April 2017.

Zivkovic, Milica. "The Double as the 'Unseen' of Culture: Toward a Definition of Doppelgänger." *Facta Universitatis,* Volume 7, Issue 2 (2000): pp. 121–128. Print.

Index

Abrams, J.J. 14, 17; see also *Fringe*
agency 8, 15, 18–20, 25, 44, 65, 67, 75, 92, 98, 112, 114–116, 121, 124, 152
aliens 19, 94–95, 122, 130–134; *see also Oblivion*
Anolik, Ruth Bienstock 30
apocalypse 15, 19, 54, 65, 73–74, 130–131
atomic bomb 157
Atwood, Margaret 44, 49
autonomy 1, 8, 15, 18–20, 25, 34, 44, 49, 65, 72, 75, 98–99, 103, 119–121, 123, 151

Bailly, Christian 140
Banks, Carolyn 30–31
Banville, John 38
Battis, Jes 66
Bay, Michael 18, 122, 154; *see also The Island*
Bedford, Robert H. 67, 69
Bennett, Betty T. 5
Bignell, Jonathan 76, 113
bioethics 34, 47, 70, 74, 125
biotechnology 13, 45, 124, 126–129, 135, 154
Blum, Joanne 21
Brake, Mark 105
Brooker, Will 143–144
Brooks, Peter 68
Burrows, David J. 22
Butler, Marilyn 31

Carroll, Rachel 44–45
Chaney, Jen 158
childhood 48
climate change 15, 65, 103
cloning 10, 13–16, 24–25, 42–50, 65–67, 69–78, 113–116, 123–130, 132–133, 143, 146, 154

Cobb, Gerald T. 35
Cojocaru, Daniel 137–138, 147
Colebrook, Claire 133
comedy 6–7, 12
The Comedy of Errors 6–7, 12
communication 3, 9–10
computers 3, 9–11, 95, 119
confession 67–68; *see also* confessional literature
confessional literature 35, 67–69
Conrad, Joseph 22–23
consciousness 14, 25, 66, 68–71, 73, 96, 101–103, 106–107, 110, 127–128, 145
crime 17, 25, 65–69, 71–73, 82–85, 117, 144, 153, 157
crime fiction 67–68
cyberpunk 87, 126
cyborg 57, 77, 93, 102, 107, 109, 146, 155; *see also* Haraway, Donna
Cylon 18, 86, 93–96, 105, 155; *see also Battlestar Galactica*

Dahlstrom, Linda 125
Daniels, Tony 52–53
Dark Matter 12–16, 20, 24, 50–58, 155
Dasen, V. 141, 144
De Camp, L. Sprague 56
de Nooy, Juliana 29–30, 81
Derry, Charles 83
Descartes, René 127
Deutsch, David 52, 59
Dewar, Elaine 69
D'Hoker, Elke 67–68
Dickens, Charles 22–23
Dietz, Frank 14, 56, 87
divorce 13, 36, 92, 118
Doctorow, Cory 43
Dolly (the sheep) 14, 43–44, 47, 114, 154; *see also* cloning
Dostoevsky, Fyodor 13, 22, 36–37, 54, 153

The Double 12–13, 16, 20–22, 24, 27, 35–41, 153–154
doubling 6–7, 10, 12–14, 24, 27–28, 32–33, 40, 44, 48–49, 70, 75, 78, 83, 99, 122, 136–137, 139, 141–149, 151–153, 155–157
drama 17, 78, 153
dreams 21, 127–130, 132, 157

economic recession 85
Egypt 2
Eminem 1
Engel, William E. 7–8
environment, role of 24, 56, 63, 76, 83, 88, 93, 116–118; see also "nature versus nurture"
The Epic of Gilgamesh 2
etymology 2, 140

Fearn, Nicholas 145
Fernbach, Amanda 108
Flood, Alison 52
Fonseca, Tony 21
Frankenstein 43
Freud, Sigmund 4, 55
Fringe 16–20, 57, 78, 86–93, 96–97, 155

game-playing 36
Garofalo, Daisy 6
Gaskell, Elizabeth 22–23
genocide 97, 148
George, Susan A. 106
Geraghty, Lincoln 93–94
Gergen, Kenneth 4, 40
Germanic folklore 4, 9
Gerrick, Christopher 7–8
ghosts 13, 24, 27–28, 31–32, 54, 152–153
Gleick, James 58
globalization 11, 93–96, 132, 134–135
Gothic literature 13, 24, 27–28, 30–33, 153
Graham, Elaine L. 4, 40, 76–79, 96, 107, 125, 140–141
Grainge, Paul 106
Greek mythology 4, 6
Grubbs, Jefferson 102–103

Haas, Elizabeth 135
Hanafi, Zakiya 141–142
Haraway, Donna 57, 77, 107; see also cyborg
Harrod, Mary Beth 68
Hayles, N. Katherine 107, 126
Heilmann, Ann 137, 148
Heller, Jason 62, 67, 70, 73
Her Fearful Symmetry 12–13, 16, 20, 24, 27–34, 81–82, 153

Hills, Matt 114
Hoben, John 131
Holliday, Christopher 131
Hood, Bruce M. 40
Horn, John 124
horror 27, 31, 46, 95, 123, 142, 144–148, 157
Huet, Marie Hélène 141
human rights 8, 18–20, 25, 43–44, 75, 78, 95, 97–100, 105, 112–121, 127, 129

imagination 2, 9, 43, 141, 146
immortality 68–70, 96
infidelity 32–33, 59–61, 139
Ingebretsen, Edward J. 140
internet, role of 3, 75, 114, 153
Iraq 93–94, 135
Ishiguro, Kazuo 12–13, 16, 20, 24, 42–50, 65, 155
The Island 16, 18–20, 78, 122–132, 135, 154
IVF 34, 114–115, 134

Jafari, Morteza 55
James, Henry 22–23, 54
Jancovich, Mark 114
Jerng, Mark 67
Jones, Nick 130, 132–133
Jones, Steve 126
Joy, Lisa 18, 98; see also Westworld
Jusino, Teresa 120

Katz, Steven T. 148
Khair, Tabish 31
Kirk, Terry 140–141
Klein, Michael J. 146
Klein, Stan 72
Kogel, Dennis 56, 87
Kolehmainen, Sophia 45
Kosinski, Joseph 19, 122, 131, 154; see also Oblivion

Labuza, Peter 148
Lafferty, Mur 12, 14–15, 20, 25, 65–74, 127, 154
Landsberg, Alison 134
Latour, Bruno 57, 77, 107
Levy, Titus 43
Liptak, Andrew 52–54
Locke, John 71, 127
Lynch, David 157; see also *Twin Peaks*; *Twin Peaks: The Return*

Madrigal, Alexis C. 34, 115
magic 19, 78, 136–143, 145–149, 156; see also *The Prestige*

The Manchurian Candidate 105; *see also* sleeper agents
Manguel, Alberto 38
Marcus, Amit 45, 67, 69, 151–152
marriage 61–62
McCarthy, Todd 133
McGowan, Todd 138, 147
medical experimentation 88, 116, 120, 154; *see also* bioethics
memory 20, 25, 48, 65–66, 70–74, 88–89, 103, 105–106, 127, 134–135
Menger, Ellen R. 109
Mesopotamia 2
Miller, William Ian 146
mirroring 7, 39, 83, 115, 117–118, 137; *see also* mise-en-abîme
mise-en-abîme 39
mistaken identity 7, 29, 31–33, 81–83, 89
Mitchell, Kaye 107
Molloy, Claire 147
"The Monster" 1
monsters 1–4, 100, 140–141
"More" 1
Morgan, Ann 33
mortality 5, 25–27, 69–70
Mullan, John 46, 48
Murray, Noel 157
music 1
mystery 15, 30, 65–68, 74, 114, 116, 136, 144

Nabokov, Vladimir 22–23
Narcissus 4; *see also* Greek mythology
nature 10–11, 18, 39, 56, 63, 112 144–145, 148
"nature versus nurture" 18, 56, 63, 112
Never Let Me Go 12–16, 24, 42–50, 65–66, 154
Niffenegger, Audrey 12–13, 20, 24, 27–34, 81, 153
Nolan, Christopher 19, 136, 143, 147, 156; *see also The Prestige*
Nolan, Jonathan 18, 98; *see also Westworld*
Norse folklore 2
Nussbaum, Emily 109–110

Oblivion 16, 19–20, 65, 78, 122–123, 130–145, 154
O'Hehir, Andrew 53
O'Keefe, Jack 103
omens 5, 129, 144
Once Upon a Time 32
ontology 18, 45–47, 70–72, 93, 98, 100, 103, 108, 116, 125–126, 133, 154–155
Opam, Kwame 107

O'Riordan, Kate 123–125, 129
Orphan Black 16, 18, 20, 78, 112–122, 154

Palmer, Dexter 12–16, 20, 25, 58–64, 155
parallel universes 59, 68, 86; *see also Dark Matter; Sliding Doors; Version Control*
Parfit, Derek 138, 144–145
Parikka, Jussi 76–77, 79
Passions 32; *see also* soap operas
Poe, Edgar Allan 6–8, 12–13, 22, 36–37, 54, 153
Pointon, Marcia 9–10
Popol Vuh 6
post-9/11 93–94, 132, 134; *see also* globalization; September 11, 2001
postcolonialism 32
post-humanism 4, 69–70, 95, 108, 116, 121, 126
postmodernism 40, 50, 75, 79, 106, 119, 126, 158
pregnancy 29, 32, 116–117, 120; *see also* reproduction
The Prestige 16, 19–20, 78, 136–149, 156
Project Leda 18, 116–122; *see also* cloning; *Orphan Black*
psychoanalytic theory 4–5; *see also* Freud, Sigmund; Rank, Otto
Puchner, Martin 46–47

Rank, Otto 4–5
rape 95, 109
Read, Rupert 138
religion 6, 23, 45, 118
Renaissance 5–8, 12, 31–32
reproduction 10, 34, 45, 47, 95–95, 112–113, 123–125, 143, 148; *see also* pregnancy
Richter, Jean Paul 12
Rihanna 1
Robinson, Joanna 101–104
Roethke, Theodore 35
Rorty, Amélie 126
"Rumpelstiltskin" 21–22
Rumsey, Abby Smith 128

sacrifice 53, 63–64, 131, 134
Schapera, I. 141, 144
Schechtman, Marya 71
science fiction 13–19, 24, 42–44, 50–53, 55–56, 58, 63, 65–69, 73–74, 78, 86–87, 91, 93, 96, 98, 104–105, 107–112, 114–116, 131, 135, 146, 154–155
Scientific Revolution 11, 141–142, 148
Seaman-Grant, Zoe E. 102–103

secrecy 14, 17, 23, 27, 29–31, 68, 70–72, 82–84, 87, 92, 103, 136, 138–139, 148
seduction 6, 32–33
Sencindiver, Susan Yi 22
September 11, 2001 11, 93–94, 132
Sexton, Anne 21–22
Shakespeare, William 6–8, 12, 18, 22, 31–33, 46
Shelley, Mary W. 5
Shelley, Percy 5
Shildrick, Margrit 126
Six Wakes 12, 14–15, 20, 25, 65–74, 127, 154
sleeper agents 94–96, 102–108; see also *Battlestar Galactica*; *The Manchurian Candidate*; *Six Wakes*; *Westworld*
Sliding Doors 54, 59
Smolenski, Phil 97
soap operas 31–32; *see also Once Upon a Time*; *Passions*
social media 3, 114
Stockly, Ed 113
Suarez, J.M. 113
suicide 17, 65, 73, 82, 94, 115–116, 135, 139, 147–148
suicide bombing 94, 135; *see also* September 11, 2001; terrorism
supernatural 10, 31, 39
superstition 5–6, 144; *see also* ghosts
suspense 83

Tallerico, Brian 157
Tally, Robert T. 7–8
technology 3, 9–11, 13–15, 18–20, 24–25, 31, 34–45, 51–61, 63–69, 74–79, 99, 101, 105–108, 119, 122–129, 131–138, 142–145, 148–149, 153, 155–157
terrorism 11, 93–94, 105; *see also* September 11, 2001; suicide bombing

Tesla, Nikola 19, 138, 142–144
time travel 56, 58, 87, 157
Toker, Leona 43–44
Torchwood 10
torture 71, 95–97, 109
tragedy 6, 36
Tsao, Tiffany 45
Turkle, Sherry 3, 75–76, 119
Twelfth Night 6
Twin Peaks 157
Twin Peaks: The Return 157

the uncanny 23, 31, 36, 55, 95, 97, 108, 129, 146; *see also* Freud, Sigmund
Updike, John 38
Usher 1

vardøger 2; *see also* Norse folklore
Vardoulakis, Dimitris 22
Version Control 12–13, 15–16, 20, 25, 56, 58–64, 155
Victorianism 31, 137

Walpole, Horace 30
Wax, Murray 142
Wax, Rosalie 142
Webber, Andrew J. 9
Westworld 16, 18, 20 78, 98–111, 155
"William Wilson" 7–8, 12–13, 36–37, 153
Williams, Linda Ruth 30, 82–83
Wolfreys, Julian 31

Yorke, John 23

Zivkovic, Milica 23–24

www.ingramcontent.com/pod-product-compliance
Lightning Source LLC
Chambersburg PA
CBHW032104300426
44116CB00007B/880